W9-BIL-216

TOP TEN GAMES YOU CAN PLAY IN YOUR HEAD, BY YOURSELF

BY J. THEOPHRASTUS BARTHOLOMEW

EDITED BY SAM GORSKI AND D. F. LOVETT

ORIGINAL ARTWORK BY GABRIEL PEREGRINO

Copyright ©2019 Corridor Digital

ISBN 978-0-9983794-1-8

All rights reserved. No part of this book may be reproduced, transmitted in any form or by any means, electronic, mechanical, photocopying, recording, or otherwise, without the prior written permission of Corridor Digital.

For Sarah and Baby Gideon.

- Sam

This is dedicated to all those who encourage and foster creativity in children—and, in particular, to the memory of my grandmothers, Beatrice and Rosemary, who each always encouraged my reading and writing.

- David

Table of Contents

FOREWORD

Sam Gorski and D. F. Lovett

WE DID NOT WRITE THIS BOOK, ALTHOUGH WE WISH WE DID.

It all began in the summer of 2014, when the two of us—Sam and David—discovered six volumes of the first edition of J. Theophrastus Bartholomew's *Games You Can Play In Your Head, By Yourself* at a yard sale in Bayport, Minnesota.

To clarify, we did not discover six copies of the book: we discovered six of the fourteen volumes of the original book series, a sprawling out-of-print game series produced by a defunct publisher in the late 1980s and early 1990s.

The books fascinated us! Here, in our hands, was something so similar to many of our favorite things—roleplaying games, tales of adventure, murder mysteries, fantasy epics—but with an entirely different approach than anything we'd seen before. Instead of gathering your friends for a night of pizza and dragon-slaying in the basement, these books urge you to isolate yourself as you dive into your own mind.

The first thing we did, of course, was divvy up the books and start playing the games ourselves. But soon we realized two things. The first was that we could find no other imprint of these games upon the world. The libraries and game stores and bookshops had all never heard of them. Even our scourings of the internet turned over no stones.

This led to our second realization: we could not keep these games from the world. But with so many volumes of games, where would we begin?

After contacting the gamemaker's publisher, we acquired a list of his ten personal favorite games, along with an introduction he had created for an unpublished volume. Ten games that challenged us. Ten games that surprised us. Ten games that changed us, for better or worse.

Again, we wish we were the authors of this book. Alas, we are but the editors. And instead of further editorializing or describing the following book, it's time for you to jump right in.

Enjoy the journey into this book... and into yourself!

Sincerely,

Sam Gorski and D. F. Lovett

INTRODUCTION

Do you remember your first daydream?

Of course you don't. No one does. To daydream is to be human, to be alive, the most natural state of existence. It is to live a separate life, to walk through other worlds, to become someone else. But in this busy, frightening, terrible world—this time and place we call America in the 1990s—you may forget not only how to daydream but that to daydream is even an option.

You are distracted by your television. Your video games. Your portable cassette players and home computers and a telephone in the kitchen that rings off the hook. All these things that scream for your attention, howling sirens drawing you to the jagged rocks of technology in the mad world that is today.

It is because of this that I have compiled a list of my ten best games. And I do mean the very best. I have created over six thousand games in my life, every one of which can be played alone. These are the absolute creams of the crop, the grandest of them all, the pinnacle of my short life's achievement.

All these games, like every game I've created, are ones that you can play in your head, by yourself. Because we are most truly ourselves—and our very best selves—when we are absolutely alone.

The Whens and the Wheres and the Whos and the Hows and the Whys

Before we jump into the games themselves, I'd like to first tell you a bit more about how to play. It is crucial that you create the kind of environment in which you can conjure up the worlds requisite for the adventures that lie ahead.

Here are the tips at their most basic:

- **Where:** First, find a solitary place, or at least where no one will bother you. This need not be an abandoned warehouse or secluded monastery. It can be as simple as your backyard or your attic or under the kitchen table. What matters is that you can be alone and that the *askers* leave you alone when you are there.
- **When:** Any time of day works. You might imagine to yourself that you can only play games alone in your head if it is recess, or after-school, or before bedtime. Any such rules are needless and frivolous. Once you go from novice to master, you can begin to play games in your head by yourself in the middle of class, while your teacher scratches at the chalkboard and your fellow students blather inanely. The sky is not the limit. The limit does not exist.
- **Where, Continued:** Sometimes the where does not have to be a place where you are alone, as noted in the **When** paragraph you just read. They say you should never blend into a crowd but sometimes, my dear friend, the crowd is exactly what you need to remain anonymous and explore new worlds. If no one is paying attention to you as an individual, then you need not pay attention to them.
- **Who:** This is the most beautiful of all the answers. If you are reading this right now then you have all the who you could ever need.
- **Why:** The question, indeed, should be why not? Do you think you can swim through this life without these games? Without the wisdom compiled for you in the book you hold right now?
- **Who, Continued:** You might think to yourself: *but what about all my friends?* To which I retort, of course, and without hesitation: *who needs them!* Do you imagine that your friends will be there for you when the sun extinguishes itself and this world ceases to exist, as it is wont to do? Will your friends be there when the pillars turn to dust and the horsemen return to town? Life is not a popularity contest. Don't kid yourself, kid. You're flying solo in these games, just like you've always been and always will be. You can go over to your friend's house and huddle around a television or squeeze onto a couch or sweat over a board game...

4

or you can close those eyes and win the Alamo for the good guys.

- **How:** Much of the how is in the following pages of this book, but there are a few things you must remember as you play these games:
    a. Find your Place of Seclusion and go there (where)
    b. Go alone (who; only you)
    c. Wear comfortable clothing
    d. Don't overthink it
    e. Breathe easy
    f. Commit fully

Now, join me as we voyage into the shadow realm, or at least to its doorstep.

The What

One of the many simple tasks required of you throughout this book is the ordinary task of fragmenting your mind to create opposing selves within yourself. This is not as daunting as it may sound at first. You do it every day.

Not sure you understand? Consider that you shape shift as you walk through the halls of your school, shifting from child to scholar to athlete to hungry beast as the bell tolls.

Or, if you are an adult who attempts to function as a cog in the blood-soaked machine we call the American Dream, consider how you swallow your own soul as you daily enter the factory where you go to die, piece by piece, five for every seven days.

Perhaps you have heard this spoken in other ways. The id and the ego and the superego; the conscious and the subconscious; the angel on one shoulder and the devil on the other; the two faces of Janus or the legions of howling demons at the door.

You might not know it, but that impulsive voice in your head—the one that tells you to push a stranger into the municipal swimming pool or to throw rocks out your bedroom window at cars passing by—is one of the many fragments of your own personality and one that will be a great ally in the games to come.

If all of this sounds daunting, confusing, or overwhelming, then let us try an exercise that will help bring some clarity to this idea.

Before you play this mini-game, go to your Place of Seclusion. Remember the tips we provided above.

The Simple Exercise That Even the Most Foolish Children Can Do

You are walking through a field. You look down and see your shadow, cast from the sun shining down on your body, darkness upon the grains of wheat, matching the outline of your body.

You know your shadow well and you always have. Your shadow walks with you, a dark reflection, a fellow self.

You reach a building here in the field. The building should be something of your choice. Conjure it up: a barn, a cottage, an abandoned house, a mill or a burned-down castle or a lonely tower.

*This is your **Sanctuary**. It beckons you. It's something special and you know it. You walk up to its front door but, as you are about to cross that threshold, something occurs to you. The shadow is not to come with you. So reach down and grab the shadow by the place it connects to your feet and pluck it off you, tossing it backward into the field.*

It is no longer just a shadow. It is now your Shadow Self.

Now, enter the Sanctuary, and begin to explore.

You are inside the Sanctuary now. It is mostly how you imagined it would be before you arrived but with some differences. Perhaps it's a bit cleaner than you thought it would be. Perhaps a bit more cluttered. Perhaps there are items of great value in here, and if not, do not worry as you still have much time to fill it.

Take a look at the objects throughout the Sanctuary, whether it's one room or a thousand. Explore until you get to know it, but remember that your Shadow Self waits outside and that it grows impatient.

Now you must play a game with your Shadow Self.

Ensure the curtains are drawn, if there are curtains. If not, ensure that your Shadow Self does not see you.

Survey the objects again. Know them.

Then, leave the Sanctuary. Go to the front door and step aside and leave the door open and nod to your Shadow Self. Let it know that its turn has come.

You will wait outside, your Human Self, as your Shadow Self goes in and explores with one simple objective: to steal an object from the Sanctuary. You cannot look in the windows, as your Shadow Self sneaks through the building with the simple purpose of tricking you. It will steal an item but, even moreso, it will rearrange the entirety of the building so that it has become an entirely new place, the same pieces but a new arrangement.

Now, pause for a moment because there is something important to remember in this game: you are both of the selves. You control each. The goal is not to trick the Shadow Self or the Human Self. The goal is to be both at once. To contain multitudes.

Wait for it, outside, your Human Self, while your Shadow Self gets into mischief.

Soon your Shadow Self will come outside again and it is your Human Self's turn to go back into the Sanctuary where you will complete one simple objective, the objective of this entire exercise: find the object the Shadow Self stole.

Go back inside and see what you have done.

Only when you have found what it was—found which object is now missing—because you stole it without letting yourself know this—there in the building you built, can you consider the game complete.

THIS SIMPLE EXERCISE IS THE FOUNDATION OF WHAT MAKES THESE GAMES POSSIBLE. BY MASTERING THIS, YOU WILL UNLOCK YOUR ABILITY TO CREATE THE WORLDS AND CHARACTERS AND EXPERIENCE THEM THROUGH THE EYES OF AN INNOCENT PLAYER.

Easy, Right?

One of the best things about all of these games is you can play them a thousand times and they will never be the same twice. If you had a hard time with the game above, try playing it again! And again!

It's not going anywhere—just like your own fractured self.

How to Explain it To Others

Surely your parents are like my own once were—distant, frowning entities with a set of stern rules, including that you should stop being a couch potato and do your damned chores.

It is hard to blame them, of course. Idle hands are indeed the playthings of Shadow Selves.

It's okay to be a couch potato. But I recommend being a couch potato with your eyes closed and the television off. That'll teach 'em!

Try it.

Speak it.

Say it aloud: "I am playing a game, Father. A game that requires you to leave me in peace and allow me to be a more fully formed human."

But then, there is something for you to remember: these are games that you play alone, by yourself, in your own head. It does not matter what the others think. What matters is that you dive into your own brain as one person and come out as another on the other side.

LET'S GO

With that, we are off. We have games to play.
And by *we*, I mean *you*.

HOW TO USE THIS BOOK

A note from the Editors

Suppose you are a plane at an airport. But where do you take off? And where are you going?

Every game is a runway, a guiding tool to point you in the right direction. When you reach the end of the runway, or chapter, it's up to you to take off.

Once you're flying, the controls are in your hands.

As you read each chapter, here are the steps you should take to ensure your gaming experience is full and complete:

1. Begin by selecting a game you want to play, or read them in the order we've placed them.
2. Read the rules for each game carefully, getting your imagination primed.
3. Then, using your imagination, envision the written events as if you are experiencing them yourself. Make it real in your head.
4. Imagine how the characters in these games will look, act, and speak.
5. Imagine how you will look, act, and speak.
6. When you see the word "GO!", that means it's time to start the game, whether you're ready or not. Close your eyes and begin imagining yourself in that story from that point forward. What happens next? What will you do?
7. Play the game until you're satisfied with its outcome.

Remember: the rules of each game are only a foundation. It is up to YOU to answer the questions posed, achieve the goals presented, and fill in any gaps you may find.

How long should I expect a game to last? That's a valid question.

Some games may last a few minutes. Others may last days or even months (it's possible for some games to last years.)

You will know when it's time to stop playing when your own story comes to an end.

One Additional Note from the Editors: Consult the Appendix for inspirations and testimonials. We have created an appendix of other experiences had by those who came before you. Feel free to flip back to it as you go for additional perspectives and thoughts.

ADVENTURE

"I've guarded this tomb for five thousand generations," whispers the skeletal jester of death who stands before you. "And none shall pass without the proper credentials."

"Last time I checked, death waits for no man," you retort. "Proper credentials be damned."

And with those words, you cast open your dusty battered cracked leather duster to reveal the six-shooter in your right hand.

Bang.

Wolves howl in the Egyptian night. Pillars of sand shake and tremble. Mummies open their eyes to see who disturbs their slumber. And an ancient malevolent clown, made of nothing but bone and gnarled skin and cobwebbed death, falls to the ground from whence he once came.

"Say hi to Ramses for me," you say. "Sucker."

Cairo. 1940. You have a treasure to find in a secret tomb... if only you can keep your hide in tact and stay one step ahead of the galley of rogues and madmen who want you dead.

13

One: Welcome to the Desert

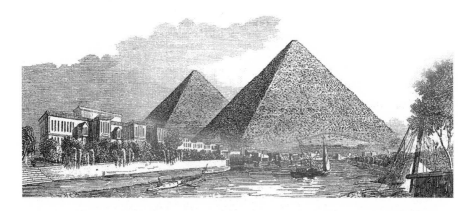

The hot winds of the Egyptian desert blow small beads of sand into your face as you step off the aeroplane. Its propeller continues to whir behind you as you hold a hand above your eyes to shelter your face from the rays of sun beating down on you.

In the distance, you can see the great pyramids. Beyond them, the city of Cairo in all its glory. Tanks roll through the city—a sign that British troops are preparing for the next phase of the great war plaguing this land.

A small man advances toward you, here in this empty land. Already you hear the sound of the aeroplane behind you resuming its frantic whirring and then disappearing as it takes off, back into the Egyptian sky.

Hassan

"I've been told that you seek a treasure," the small man says. "And that this treasure is in a forbidden tomb."

You do not answer the small man. Not yet. He wipes his brow again and looks around, as if someone in this empty desert could hear the words he speaks.

"I have a serious question for you," he continues. "What is the tomb you seek? And why?"

"The tomb I seek," you mutter. "The tomb I seek…"

And so, Adventurer, it's time to determine your answer: what tomb? What treasure? And why?

Two: The Adventurer

YOU ARE AN ADVENTURER. ONE WHO ADVENTURES. THIS MUCH IS KNOWN.

However, there are many sorts of Adventurers in this world. It's important for you to decide what sort you are: if you're a good guy or a bad guy. If you seek fame or fortune, diamonds or golds, death or immortality.

In order to build your Adventurer, it's important that you ask and answer the following questions:

MAN OR WOMAN?

A simple question and a good starting point. Are you a man or a woman? Game players often feel limited to playing as their own birth gender, which is a needlessly limiting approach.

Age?

It's important that you have a clear idea of how old you are. It's common, when creating Adventurers, to choose ones in the ostensible prime of their lives. While this can be fun, it often depletes the challenge...unless you seek to craft an Adventurer whose ultimate lesson is in the hubris of youth and the empty glory of physical strength.

Choose if you'd like to play as a teen, a young adult, a middle-aged man, or an Adventurer reaching an older stage of life. Any of these are acceptable, but this should not be taken lightly: as we move forward with this game, you'll increasingly learn that the vast account of your Adventurer's life experiences are relevant to the Adventure at hand.

AMERICAN OR NAZI?

You're either a red-blooded American who likes killing Nazis, or you're a Nazi. The two most opposing forces there are. No Nazi could ever be an American and no American could ever be a Nazi. Those are the facts.

Assuming that you are not a Nazi in real life—and if you are, pal, then I've got a knife I'd like to introduce to your throat—it's probably a tough idea to empathize with such a character.

Why would you play as a Nazi? Well, it can be more interesting to play as a villainous character. It alters your motives, your worldview, your very understanding of the game you play.

Remember one more detail: if you choose to play as a Nazi, there are only two fitting ends to your story: redemption or death.

Occupation?

Obviously, we know that you are a person with a bug for Adventure. But how do you butter your bread? What keeps your lights on? What is your day job?

If you're a Nazi, then there's a good chance that you're involved in either the military or politics.

Other potential occupations include professor, scientist, diplomat, museum curator, librarian, associate professor, professor emeritus, or adjunct professor.

Motivated by Gold, Justice, Truth, or Immortality?

What drives you? Answer carefully, and perhaps not immediately.

What is it that you wish to find on this Adventure? Riches and wealth? Vengeance? The death of your enemies or, at least, the weapons with which to kill them? The salvation of the world? The cure for death and disease, whether yours or someone else's?

Human or Ghoul?

Perhaps this option did not occur to you. Have you assumed yourself to be human this entire time? A safe assumption, usually, and a safe way to play during your first round.

But consider the motivations of a ghost or a ghoul or an unworldly, inhuman creature, seeking out a tomb in another land. Are you up to such an Adventure? Perhaps you are a vengeful spirit that occupies a mortal husk to do your bidding? Perhaps you are both man and blood demon?

Magic or Not?

One more thing that you may not have considered is the possibility that you possess magic powers. This is also not recommended for the novice, as magic can go haywire and cause some terrible trouble. There are also few things more dangerous than a Nazi Sorcerer, so tread lightly before jumping into playing as such a character.

Is your character coming into focus? Do you know who you are yet?

Perhaps you think you know exactly who you are. What you want. But let's explore all the options.

We have touched on your motivations above but there is still much to determine. In particular, we must consider your mission.

Three: The Tomb You Seek

There are lots of tombs in Cairo and basically all of them are haunted. If you're wondering why so many of these tombs are haunted, it's pretty simple: tombs have dead people in them and when those dead people are disturbed, you get hauntings.

As stated above, your humble Egyptian guide, Hassan, would like to have a better understanding of how he can help you. If he is to do this, it's important for you to know exactly what you seek.

A TOMB OF BLOOD MAGIC AND IMMORTALITY

Almost every crypt is haunted for the simple reason stated above: dead people.

But some of these crypts are darker.

Consider, for example, the case of Thrazzakes the Dark Lord. In this case, you're not talking so much about a tomb but, instead, about a place where a Lord of blood magic has been trapped for millenia, brooding and pacing and waiting for the day he's unleashed upon this world once again.

Remember to consider who you are before thinking about how you would interact with such a place. If you are a rogue Nazi, a scoundrel who respects no one and nothing beyond the villains to whom you report, you might find something appealing in the idea of harvesting a Dark Lord's power. It could also quickly make you and your cronies entirely irrelevant.

If you are an American civilian, a noble professor, a gallivanting noblewoman, then perhaps you seek this tomb for a noble reason. But, be warned: once you unlock the tomb and step across its threshold, you will be stirring up a storm of hellish beings and non-beings.

A TOMB OF HAUNTED RICHES

There are many tombs in this world. Tombs of wealth, of coins, of diamond brooches and ruby-encrusted daggers. So much gold. <u>So much delightful gold!</u>

Many times, these tombs of gold coins, of silver armor, of unicorn wands and magic helms and sacred medallions will be guarded by keepers of the coin. Mummies, perhaps, lurking in the darkness. Or lichs. Or other shape-shifting beings, believing themselves to be the entity whose purpose it is to keep people like you from getting your grubby hands all over their ancient riches.

Like tombs of blood magic and the crouching undead, tombs of haunted riches also contain great risks with terrible promise.

The assumption that any tomb of haunted riches will be beneath a pyramid is <u>correct</u>.

> *A Note from the Editors: Sometimes your Adventure may lead you away from a pyramid. That is OK. As you determine the mission you're on, don't limit yourself by your own assumptions.*

A TOMB OF ANCESTRAL SECRETS

Perhaps you seek something more than the deathbox of a caged beast or the stolen inheritance of a prince who only wishes to sleep. Perhaps what you seek is something deeper, something more personal.

Do you seek something related to your own personal history? Do you seek to learn about what happened there? The place where an ancestor is buried? A place where a great-great-grand-uncle was buried alive with a family heirloom that you must recover? The place where your once noble family fell from glory, your wealth and possessions buried away from the light of man?

A TOMB OF HOPE FOR HUMANITY

Sometimes it's a matter of blood magic. Of crouching darkness. Of creatures as powerful as a firebombing.

Other times it's the exact opposite. It's something that holds the keys to a new world. Peace. Love. Something that will lead our whole human race to lay down our weapons.

Imagine such a thing, an anti-weapon. A device, a talisman, an entity so powerful that it will open our eyes, the eyes of all people so that we see who we could be, who and what we could become if we believed in something better. Something bigger. Remember that you are in Cairo in 1940. What horrors go on in this world, not far from where you stand? What can you do to end them?

If you seek a tomb like this, ask yourself: do you seek it for noble reasons? For ignoble reasons? Do you wish to use the anti-weapon?

Or do you intend to destroy it?

But We Aren't Done Yet...

If there are any aspects of your identity that remained unclear to you until now, go back to your character traits and imagine, again, who it is that you are. Perhaps it's becoming clearer now that you know what it is that you seek.

Four: The Troubling Childhood Memory You Repeatedly Relive

One central aspect of your character should be a defining moment from your early life, presumably your pre-adolescence or early adolescence, that still haunts you today. Please note that this is not the Adventure itself, but it can largely inform the quest that you are now on, the way you approach it, and how your enemies may try to manipulate you.

The Sudden, Tragic Death of a Beloved Pet or Relation

What child does not have such a memory?

Go beyond the obvious, if you choose this as backstory. Go deeper, into something more troubling, more sudden or drawn-out. You are more than a grown man who once, as a boy, saw his prized horse shot in the head when its colic became too much. If you had a horse, and the horse had colic, then you are the one who executed it and you executed it in a way that still surprises you. You are not a tender-footed smiling hero. Whether good or evil, you are an Adventurer who runs with a demon on your back.

A Supernatural Experience in a Gothic Manor

Did you once visit a distant relation's manor or abbey, somewhere north of London or Luxembourg or in the darkened forests of Germany or Vermont? Did they ignore you, the older relatives, leaving you to fend for yourself? And did you find yourself unable to sleep, certain you heard the wails of a woman or child locked in an attic or a Dungeon? These creaks and squeaks still haunt you.

Perhaps this blends in with the memory above. Few things haunt a child more—even in his or her grown days—than a walk amongst tombstones, unable to see over the hills of the graves or the moss-covered stones themselves. Maybe you saw a ghost or, more likely, maybe you spent your entire time in the graveyard certain that you were about to. Perhaps you still wake on nights both hot and cold remembering when you thought you would die in that place and stay there a ghost forever.

Or, perhaps, you wonder if this is indeed what happened and if you are nothing more than a wandering ghoul to this day.

AN UNREQUITED SUMMER ROMANCE WITH A COQUETTISH NEIGHBOR

As a child, blossoming into young adulthood, did you meet a sprite of a lass or a charming boy with sun-golden hair and fall into orbit—only to have your heart broken when he or she did not feel the same way? Did you weep at night? Did you lose your appetite? Did you long for the touch of your love who did not feel even the slightest reciprocation to your longing?

A REQUITED YET ULTIMATELY TRAGIC ROMANCE WITH A COQUETTISH NEIGHBOR

Or perhaps they loved you back? And did this make it hurt all the more?

THE FINDING OF A PECULIAR, FRIGHTENING TALISMAN

Did you find something in an antique store? Maybe a monkey's paw or gilded porcelain tea cup? Did you put it in your pocket? Carry it with you? Hold it close? And did it turn out to have some terrible power that haunted and twisted you, turning you into something very unlike yourself?

And did you destroy this talisman? Or do you carry it with you today?

Five: Let's Travel Through Cairo

You know who you are.

You know what you seek.

And you know what haunts you.

The question is how will you find the tomb you seek?

If you want to succeed, you are going to have to find the right resources and surround yourself with the right people.

"So, tell me," your small guide says. "Tell me about this tomb."

Monologue

Briefly, considering the entirety of your backstory and character motivations that you have just selected, explain yourself to the guide. Keep it snappy as you explain, as this guy is paid by the day and you really shouldn't waste much more time on backstory when you have a treasure to find.

So, tell him all about it and, when you're finished talking, look at him and wait for a response.

The Guide's Response

He looks at you sideways. It seems, for a moment, as if he wonders if he can trust you. If he suspects you are playing a trick or an elaborate joke on him.

Then he snaps out of it and begins to speak.

"I do not know the exact location of the place you seek," he says, whispering now as he looks around again. "But I can tell you that it is very dangerous."

Consider what you have to say to that. It's probably something about how you knew you signed up for danger.

But then he adds: "there is something else. But I cannot tell you about it here. We must go into the city and I will show you."

Six: The Speakeasy

There, he says. You are not the only one who seeks treasures and crypts. And there is another one of your seekers across the bar. Your competition in this race.

As you size them up from across the smoke-filled speakeasy, watch them drink a drink appropriately matched to their personality, you whisper to Hassan, **"Tell me who I'm looking at."**

Choose Your Antagonist

Luis Ortega

"You might know him," says Hassan. "The Spanish claim he's a turncoat who joined the Nazis. The Nazis accused him of being a spy for the Americans. The Americans said they've never heard of him—aside from the tycoon Chatsworth Chan, who hired him to find his child when the boy was abducted."

This information likely jogs your memory: you met Ortega, once, somewhere between one and ten years ago. Imagine where it was. Picture his swagger, his laugh, and the rude, dismissive thing you said to him.

You are not here for vendettas—but maybe, just maybe, seeing Ortega here will give you reason to move faster. To spare not another moment.

Lady Evelyn Canary

"I'm sure you recognize her from the newspapers," he says. "The devil in the white dress. The widow thricefold. The demon of Dover."

You indeed have read about her. A lady of the first degree, with several dashes of villainy. Once the piano-playing prodigy of the mine-owning Wellington family from the south of Dover, Evelyn Wellington made waves and headlines when she abandoned her family fortune to elope with Sultan Sebastian Canary of the Kingdom of Fennario. The Sultan died shortly afterward when he and Lady Evelyn were seeking some buried treasure off the coast of Bermuda—since his death, she's spent his fortune seeking further tombs and is now running low on funds.

Her favorites are rubies and diamonds, although Lady Evelyn is not picky. Her weakness is not only the treasures but the chase itself.

THE GHOST

"_____ _____"

You hear your name spoken, as if by a ghostly apparition.

Hassan, meanwhile, will begin to describe a third potential antagonist, but his whispers go in one ear and out the other. Whomever he is identifying as the third competitor racing to the tomb matters not because a Troubling Childhood Memory interferes with your perception of reality.

"_____ _____"

You hear your name called out, again. As Hassan's words fade from your senses, your blood runs cold. Your spine twists and tingles.

You don't know how you didn't see her before but there, sitting across the bar from you, is the cruelest person you've ever met. Your childhood tormentor. The bully you almost forgot.

It's none other than a phantom of your wicked, villainous step-sister. You whisper her name:

"___ _____"

What is she doing here, you think. How did she find me?

What does she want?

Or perhaps you never had a step sister and this is the work of an ancient spirit. Who knows?

Seven: The Master Mapmaker

"We need to move now," Hassan says. "With your antagonist here, it means they have not yet found the Master Mapmaker."

Whether you've already heard of the Master Mapmaker or not, it's pretty easy to figure out what his job is. No intelligent questions to ask about this.

And so you race from the speakeasy into the bright lights of the desert city, following Hassan through the busy streets. When you reach him, the Mapmaker, you tell him what it is that you want. What you've come from and what you seek.

"Yes, yes, yessssss," the Mapmaker says. "Yes, I was warned of you by the spirits and the demons who sit on my shoulders while I draw these maps."

"You have demons and spirits who sit on your shoulders while you draw maps?" Hassan looks startled as he speaks. "I didn't know that. Should we go find a different Mapmaker?"

"I am the best one there is," the Master Mapmaker says. "Only I know. Only I have had the visions of the dark labyrinths and traps that reside within the pyramids, your eventual destination. Only I can draw you the map you need to find the tomb you seek."

"Then give it to us."

"It will cost you something," the Mapmaker says.

"Everything has a cost," says Hassan. "Just hand it over and we can deal with the cost later."

And so he hands it to you:

> A MAP OF THE LABYRINTHS BENEATH THE PYRAMIDS.

The Hunt is On

Map in hand and servant in tow, you're finally ready to delve into the depths of the Pyramids. You arrive at the base of the greatest of the Pyramids and the entrance to the twisting labyrinth within it, and unfurl your map:

How strange. The map admittedly looks a little... lacking. But quickly you realize it will be up to you to compete the map, as this is your imagination, and the complexity of the labyrinths will be completely up to you.

25

With the help of your Shadow Self, generate the structure of the labyrinth and the traps and secrets within it.

The sand stings your cheeks with each gust.

With map in hand you step before the great pyramids, ready to forge a path to riches or ruin.

Do you dare Adventure?

GO!

SHADOWS AND TREASURES #1

An Interlude

Breathe. Return to your senses. Return to your life. It's still you, here, the same soul and skin as before.

You might not feel like it, of course. You might still imagine yourself to be in a distant land, across chasms and schisms, a hero or villain who found a tomb and the horrors or dreams it contained.

Before we jump into the next game—and boy, is it a crazy one— let's unpack our adventuring bag and consider what we learned.

THE SANCTUARY

You recall, of course, the simple game we played in the introduction. It may feel as if it was ages ago, considering you just spent some time in Cairo in the 1940s.

Remember? You walked through a field and found an empty place, walls and a roof that you entered and explored. You set your Shadow Self loose in that place.

Return now, to that place, be it a cottage or a tower or a Dungeon. Your Sanctuary is your place where you go to breathe, to relax, to recharge before next game.

Return to it, with your Shadow Self beside you.

Stand outside and look upon it.

Now, step forward, with both you and yourself, and enter the building.

THE BOX OF TREASURES

There is something that waits for you in this house. There, in the corner. Do you see it?

It's a box, or perhaps a chest, or perhaps a safe.

Walk up to it. Look at it. Touch it with your hands and get to know the feel of it, whether gilded copper or rusted steel or scratched oak or anything else that you might imagine this treasure box to be.

Open it. It's unlocked.

Look inside and see that it is empty. For now.

WHAT WILL YOU PUT IN THE TREASURE BOX?

This box, it belongs to you. It is for you to put your treasures in, the things you find and keep when you play these games.

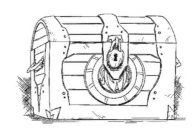

So far, you have played one game. It is up to you what you choose to add, but I will tell you what I have found and what, if you played correctly, I'd assume you found too.

I have played Adventure hundreds of times. Here are a few of the things I've discovered:

✓ **A bejeweled undead beetle** that spent a thousand years in a glass box before I uncovered it
✓ **The mummified paw of a large cat**—or, perhaps, a cat-handed human
✓ **A small vial of magic blood**
✓ **A pair of large rainbow feathers** that give me the ability of flight

What you place in your Treasure Box is up to you.

Before you play the next game, spend some time here in your Sanctuary and determine what it is that you will add to your treasure box. Feel free to record what you place in the box in the NOTES section at the end of this book.

READY?

Another game awaits us. Are you ready to take the leap?

SPACE

YOUR GLOVED HAND REACHES OUT FOR A GLOWING RED
BUTTON.

You press it firmly. Two large docking bay doors in front of you
shudder, and a crack forms between them as light from the M829 Nebula
sears a glowing white line into your eyes. It's brilliant: A tandem set of
stars has just collided and has set off a premature supernova. Best part?
You've got front row seats, complete with a full bottle of Tarkovian Spice
Wine running through your in-suit hydration system and a packet of fatty
sustenance capsules for snacking.

Quonk, a two-foot tall Uhlvidian Warrior-Toad gives you a
knowing nod from the back of the docking bay.

"I got the helm, Cap'n, if you's thinking about going for a stroll."
he says.

No doubt he and the crew will be getting rowdy while you're
offdeck. But would you expect any less from the motley crew you've
assembled? Such is the life of a Space-pirate captain like yourself. You
have earned your Ship, your reputation. And now you've earned some
time off.

So you step out into the nothingness. The momentum of that
single step is enough, sending you flying towards the dazzling abyss. It
turns out that those two stars once were home to nearly 1000
civilizations. And now, dust.

You're floating. No, flying. Surrounded by blues of dying stars and greens of gaseous clouds. You feel weightless, because in Space there is no gravity. So it's more than a feeling. It's for <u>real</u>!

Travel Outer Space in your Space Ship!

It Is Time To Ascend

SPACE. IT'S HAPPENING ALL AROUND US.

Everyone has always been curious about what's in Outer Space. You've likely found yourself on a back porch at some point, gazing up into the night sky, interrogating your own self about the depths of our cosmos with questions such as:

What is going on in Space?

and

How far away is it?

and

If presented with the opportunity to travel to Space, which planet would I choose to go to?

Furthermore, propelling one's self into the great beyond would be cleansing and enlightening. All the baggage that keeps you here on Earth—your house, your belongings, your friends and family—would be shed as you started anew.

And so it is my aim to answer these questions and explore these possibilities by sending you on a journey to the stars. Today you will travel into the cosmos.

Rid yourself of your Earthly desires and upgrade to new Universaly desires! Fare thee well, sweet traveler!

Your Garage, The Present

Your garage, right now.

Your story begins on Earth. Your city. Your street. Your block. Your home. Your garage. And inside that garage (a tiny place which is dwarfed when compared to the size of the universe) awaits your monumental creation.

With great pride you walk up to the back door of that garage. With a jingle, you take out your keyring to unlock the many layers of padlocks that secure the door shut. Since it will take a few minutes to unlock them all, you spend that time mulling over the years of toiling and tinkering that have birthed your invention. You finally jimmy open the door and turn on the light switch to reveal...

...your SPACE SHIP! The first Space Ship capable of intergalactic travel. Its hull glimmers under the dim light bulb that hangs in the center of the garage. It amazes you that you've been able to build it all on your own, and that your local hardware store had the supplies to construct the vast majority of it. You slap the hood of the newly minted vessel: it feels pretty solid. Solid enough for Space travel!

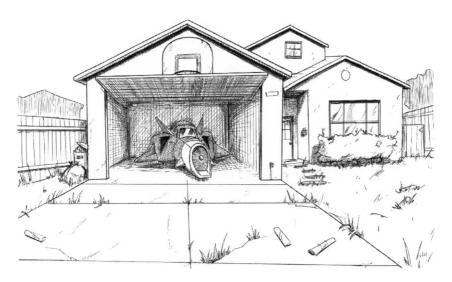

My Very Own Space Ship

There are two incredible aspects to your invention: firstly, it's small enough to fit in your garage, and secondly, it only seats one.

It's time to conceive and construct your SPACE SHIP. Take a moment to walk around your garage and observe all aspects and angles of the craft. Be sure to document it in great detail.

What features have you installed? What color is it? What materials is it primarily constructed from? Are you proud of it? Where have you installed your Navigation Computer? You'll need to use it to find your way around Space.

How Does It All Work?

You may be asking yourself, I just don't buy it. A Space Ship? In my garage?

Now, it sounds a little far-fetched—but trust me—it's not. If you need an explanation of how you discovered or invented the plans to create it, or simply refuse to believe that this story you're in is true, then feel free to skip this game and try something easier.

Why don't you skip on down to the library and read one of those books where all the stories are planned out for you?

HOWEVER:

If you are standing in your garage looking at your SPACE SHIP right now, **continue**.

Keeping Your Agenda *Under Wraps*

"I just don't buy it. A bonafide Space Ship. In your garage?" is also a question that others might ask you if you mistakenly reveal your creation to them. It's worth mentioning that attempting to explain how your SPACE SHIP works to anyone will simply confound them, so it's best to keep this project *under wraps*. Only you will ever truly understand its inner workings.

Keeping your project *under wraps* will protect the integrity of the Craft from peepers and tinkerers. One screw gets loose and the whole Ship might go ka-boom upon liftoff. Also, because this technology is one of a kind, there are many jealous, evil men out there who may attempt to steal your technology, plans, or the entire Craft itself.

It's Time For Liftoff!

"Hold on just one minute! I'm not yet ready to take flight!" you say aloud. "I've only just accustomed myself to this Space Craft, and I barely know the controls! Besides... I've still got business on Earth!"

You fidget at the what you think is the door of the Space Craft, unable to encapsulate yourself within its airtight hull.

Eventually your mind comes to a conclusion:

"Perhaps I need a purpose or destination to fly towards."

Liftoff will commence once you are confident to fly, so do not rush yourself into Space travel. ✒

Here's what a typical **liftoff sequence** entails:

1. Decide what business you have in Space. Before embarking on a mission that may last the entire duration of your life, consider creating a plan of action, or setting a goal for yourself. Don't worry about the exact physical destination; that comes later.
2. Relinquishing your Earthly possessions. Do you have pets that must be given away? Do you have a roomates who can sell your items in a garage sale? Perhaps finding a storage unit will help. (Remember: if you are going to enlist help from your roommates, in selling your Earthly possessions, you must still keep your purpose and agenda *under wraps*.)
3. Securely fastening yourself inside your Space Ship. What kind of seat or chair have you installed in the bridge of your Star Ship? Ships travel fast and you don't want to be left behind!
4. Programming a destination into your Navigation Computer. Which planet or celestial object that's relevant to your Space Business do you wish to travel towards?
5. Hitting the "GO" button on your Space Ship's control console. Which button does what on your control console? **Don't worry, there's no wrong answers.**

Feeling confident yet, Captain? All of these steps are simple and straightforward, and you should be able to accomplish them easily on your own.

If you are still not ready to enter Space, that's completely normal. Let's solve that. **Now.**

What Business Do You Have In Space?

says JEFF, your Navigation Computer. But you're not paying attention, instead reading the latest e-Zines from Station 8. Moments later you look up and realize your mistake!

"JEFF, set us back on course! Recorrect!" you demand. But to no avail...

Unfortunately you still turn off too late, and guess what happens next? Your Ship spins out of control, and now you're stuck in a black hole!

Space is so vast that one wrong turn and you'll be lost forever, twirling through the cosmos like a leaf in the autumn wind. This is why it's crucial that you figure out what business you have up there so you'll have something to guide your journey.

If you're not sure what business you have in Space, choose one of the following business opportunities that take you to Space:

I Want To Make a Map Of Space

Your meticulous personality is exactly what the cartographer of the known universe needs. Planet to planet you wish to go, documenting each and every feature you see, hoping one day to provide a comprehensive map for travellers yet to come.

How Far Into Space Can I Go?

You've always been known for your competitive spirit, and that's a perfect match for this one-of-a-kind adventure into the farthest reaches of our starscape. So with your hands off the steering wheel and your throttle set to full, you're right on your way to setting a world record for "Person to Travel The Farthest Away From Earth".

How deep does Space go? Only you will find out.

I Think I'm An Alien

You've always known you're different, and not just because of how your face looks. A feeling deep within you your whole life has told you that you're destined for a higher purpose and the answers don't lie here on Earth. But you won't be able to know for sure until you get into Space, because you've never met or seen an Alien before, and until you do, you can't confirm your suspicions.

I No Longer Wish To Live On Earth

Earth is just one of many planets in the universe, and chances are that another planet may suit your lifestyle better. Whether you're in a rut or just looking for something new, no longer wishing to live on Earth is completely normal.

I Am Looking For An Alien To Be My Friend

Always a loner, you've been eager to meet someone who you can finally call your friend. After an exhausting search on Earth and plenty of failures, you've come up empty handed and are ready for your next stop: Space.

More specifically, a place in Space where a friendly Alien lives.

Just A Quick Jaunt

You've always been content with your life on Earth, but since you just poured years into the creation of a Space Ship, you can't resist taking it out for a little spin. Maybe do some donuts around the moon when nobody is watching? Or fish tail and drift across Saturn's rings?

You may wish to wear a mask to hide your face in case any nosy Earthlings see you through their telescope and wonder who you are (since you're keeping things *under wraps*).

But keep in mind: once you're done, you're headed straight back home.

Using The Navigation Computer

An example of a JEFF system.

You've finally run the extension cord from your house to your garage, and that means your Navigation Computer finally has power! The display comes to life with equations, rudimentary maps of the stars, and charts of data all rapidly loading and scrolling.

Only one question left: where to?

Your Navigation Computer is your portal to other worlds. The technicalities of Space flight are too advanced for human hands, so it's best left up to a processor like the one you've just installed.

Your Navigation Computer, or JEFF, depending if you've named it JEFF, responds either by voice commands or typing directly onto his keyboard.

WHAT IS SPACE?

Outer Space is defined as the void between us and the answers that lie in the cosmos. Very little is known about Outer Space. Before we force upon you such a difficult task of discovering and exploring it on your own, you need to orient yourself towards the discoveries you may make.

Before travelling into Space, it's crucial that you understand exactly what you're getting yourself into. Here are the three theories on what Space is, exactly, and how they may shape the journey you've chosen to embark on:

Note: You need to decide <u>one</u> version of Space to play.

---

1. A DIVERSE ECOSYSTEM OF INTELLIGENT ALIEN LIFE

The fungal noodles created by a five eyed chef on Saborious 7. The risque late night holo shows playing on Space Station Zeeble. The quaint Quadro Colonies set in the red grass fields of Mars.

There is certainly a possibility that other intelligent life exists in the universe: a colorful array of charismatic companions, callous conflicts, and cunning consciousness that may exceed even our own comprehension. In this optimistic view, boundless exploration is for you to behold, finding perhaps a greater life than you had here on Earth.

What new clues lead us to the origin of life in the universe? What civilizations are there to meet? What is your role, and the role of Earthen peoples, in this universal nation of beings?

2. A HUMAN CENTRIC VIEW OF THE UNIVERSE

Just beyond our solar system lies a vast array of rocks, gasses, and ecosystems that have yet to evolve past a primordial goo. As your Star Ship glides through the blackness, you quickly find the silence of the universe is deafening. You find yourself to be the only person wherever you go. Time passes you by as you scan for lifeforms to no avail. The universe has never felt so small.

Humans are the dominant life form in the universe. They are now and forever will be. It becomes quite clear that God, or a god, has chosen Earth as its crowning masterpiece. So, not all is lost. You still may find something interesting out there, but don't expect to get into any shenanigans with Aliens and whatnot.

Earth is an oasis in a desert of nothing.

Perhaps there are Space anomalies out there that we have yet to observe? Or even better, perhaps you will find a vein of valuable minerals on a distant planet, and concoct a plan to convert them into unimaginable wealth back on Earth? Perhaps you will feel an urge to colonize another planet, which is entirely normal in this situation.

3. REALITY IS A SIMULATION

Your Star Ship takes off, rocketing through the atmosphere! That's when things get weird. Time stutters. The laws of physics and matter become inconsistent. And just as you reach the edge of our solar system, about to cross into the great unknown, your Star Ship freezes.

The thin veneer which is the edge of the simulation we inhabit has been reached, and the universe as we know it is but a backdrop, a star-patterned programmed wallpaper to make us believe that our lives serve a greater purpose.

With your dreams dashed, you glumly turn your Star Ship around and head back to Earth to wrestle with your findings. But along the way you may realize that whoever is running this simulation might be doing so for a reason. A noble reason.

What would they be trying to learn from this experiment called Humanity?

And if our perception of reality is a lie, what is the true universe that our simulation resides in?

Surely whoever is running this simulation has restricted our parameters of experience—and in true reality we would be able to achieve much more.

Which forces you to ask, what is real? What isn't real?

Is our reality modeled after theirs? Will someone please give us a sign that we're doing a good job being humans? Please?

TIME FOR LIFTOFF, part 2

Now that you've gotten a hold of your Space Ship, figured out your business in Space, and of course, decided what Space actually is, you're finally ready to travel to Space.

There's not really much else to add. You just have to get out there.

> Ultimately, no one really knows very much about Space, so you'll have to figure out what it's like when you get there.

Business? Decided.

Under wraps? Check.

Possessions? Relinquished.

My body? Securely fastened.

Destination? Programmed.

"GO" button? My finger is at the ready, waiting to press it.

GO!

SHADOWS AND TREASURES #2

An Interlude

Here we are again.

Look up to the sky. And if you're inside, find a window.

See that shining star? That's you! Flying to the stars and beyond.

Who knew what visions could apparate within your waking mind?

Of course, like before, take a moment to return to your Sanctuary.

Put something in your Treasure Box. Something you may have found on another planet, or even a frost-covered moon. Something you discovered and brought back with you after your time in Outer Space. (Even just the keys to your Space Ship will work, if you have yet to take off for some reason.)

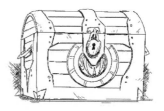

Something only you know. Something for just you.

Don't forget to look out for more treasures in these upcoming games!

Won't it be amazing to one day look back at these treasures and reminisce of the adventures you once had? Who knows what fun souvenirs might lurk in the deep dark Dungeons, or on the open road?

DUNGEONS

CASTLE DAGON RISES IN THE DISTANCE,

a crack of lighting silhouetting it against the night rain. From the shadows, a young Adventurer marches towards it: Aelon, the last surviving Warrior-Toad of Uhlvidia.

She wipes her soaked blonde hair from her brow to get a better look at the Dungeon for which she heads but, unfortunately, she can see only the castle. The Dungeon is yet to come—unseeable, unknowable, hidden below ground.

Judging by the size of the castle, Aelon imagines the Dungeon beneath it must be miles deep. Traversing it would take months to complete. To explore it would test all her resolve—the bards say this Dungeon's size is matched only by its sadistic creativity.

And so Aelon trudges forward through the mud and windswept lands to the great Castle Dagon. What secrets await beneath its ground? What characters will she find imprisoned in such a gargantuan network of horrors? Will this Dungeon be worth her time? Will she reach its end before reaching her own end?

Experience the Dungeon-themed Adventure of a lifetime! Concoct a Dungeon-full of exciting traps and secrets and enemies, then forge through it as an Adventurer trapped within it or as a keeper of the Dungeon or as one of the prisoners or as simply the Lord who had it commissioned in the first place, pleased with whatever handiwork you contributed.

MY PERSONAL RELATIONSHIP WITH DUNGEONS

AND

THE PURPOSE OF THIS GAME

-An aside-

I have written a special introduction for this game because I need you to know how important it is. There are two purposes for this particular game.

The first is simple: play the game.

The second is to play in a way that allows you to elevate the respect Dungeons receive in today's society. Dungeons are underestimated and under-appreciated these days, but not necessarily in the way one might think. Even amongst those who speak the word *Dungeon* the most—those who gather around card tables in basements, who isolate themselves into pockets of four or five in the school cafeteria, who war against dragons in their brave little bands—there is no emphasis *on* or enthusiasm *for* Dungeons themselves.

That is what has driven me to create this game and what I want you to get out of it. Not just a fun adventure, but the desire and the ability to construct a decent Dungeon of your own.

So I must ask a question before we begin. You do not have to answer it... yet.

Are you capable of conceiving and constructing a sprawling Dungeon, memorizing each and every corner and trap and also the greater world with each rhyme and reason for which it exists, all within the confines of your mind and memory?

Take a moment to imagine an iceberg, if you will. Surely, you are familiar
with those behemoths of the sea: icebergs. A castle is to land as an iceberg is
to the sea, with the castle on top and the vast Dungeon below. Most castles
were designed to be nearly 60% Dungeon, as lawlessness and treachery ran
rampant during medieval life.

Dungeons

Midnight strikes. Now inside Castle Dagon, Aelon the roguish Uhlvidian toad woman creeps through the throne room, knowing full well that the entrance to the Dungeon is somewhere near here. Hidden, and she must find it.

She looks behind the throne, a common place for secret stairwells. Not there.

Perhaps pulling on this wall torch will reveal... no, not there either. Where is this blasted Dungeon?

"Explain yourself, toad." a voice echoes.

Aelon gasps and turns to see the King, sword in hand.

"I seek your Dungeon, and the gold within it!" she demands.

The King raises his sword. "The lizard woman is blind. She does not see. The very walls that surround us are my Dungeon and as such you are now my prisoner," the King replies.

"Your... prisoner?!" the words slip from Aelon's lips. Confounded, she thinks to herself, "What does he mean, 'Dungeon'? I could have sworn this was the <u>throne room.</u> The banners on the wall, the throne, the king. I must surely reconsider what I call a Dungeon if I'm to escape with my life."

What is a Dungeon?

You don't know, do you? That's fine. No one does.

Take a moment and attempt to define, in your mind, that crucial word: *Dungeon.*

Hold it in your mind: *Dungeon.*

Make it your mantra: *Dungeon.*

Whisper it as you lie in bed awake counting to yourself:

Dungeon.

Dungeon.

Dungeon.

Now I repeat the question: what is a Dungeon?

We take for granted the all-too common representations of them. Cobblestone, yes. Torchlight, yes. Glorified brick-laden basements of humble rural abodes, yes.

A traditional, uninspired Dungeon.

But Dungeons can also be the ancient catacombs of phantasmagoric cathedrals. Dungeons can be natural cave formations, turned into mines, turned once again into bases for wily goblins. Dungeons can even be the innards of a behemoth, with flesh for walls and cascading stomachs and digestive tracts to explore.

Consider the Dungeons that exist today. Take, for example, a modern day cell block. Oppressive iron bars enabling the imperialist tradition of slavery. Cage after cage of imprisoned drug dealers and thieves, held in captivity for their failings (and the failings of their unflinching society).

Stretch your imagination further! A Dungeon can be an uncomfortable family gathering where you are forced into conversation with a distant relation whose breath reeks of stale wine, but you cannot leave since you are trapped, just like your school cafeteria or physical education class are also Dungeons.

Like Aelon the toad woman learned in our story above, we now know Dungeons are not always what we expect.

Ultimately, Dungeons are any area designed to trap and imprison living beings. They can take many forms, but generally they have four walls, a roof, a floor, and an entrance that can be sealed or locked. The material and location do not matter.

You will have to shed your expectations and limitations if you are to escape the Dungeon of your enemies... or design the Dungeons of your dreams.

What isn't a Dungeon?

After broaching the topic of Dungeons to some respected colleagues, it has come to my attention that there are in fact some things which are not Dungeons.

These are <u>not</u> Dungeons:

➤ Porches and gazebos.
➤ Small things that move (cars, carriages, wagons, boats, trains)
➤ Outside
➤ Roofs
➤ Fenced-off areas
➤ Coned-off areas
➤ Shaded areas
➤ Cages (although cages can be in Dungeons)
➤ Trenches, Pits, and Holes
➤ Nets
➤ Boxes
➤ Water (except when turned to ice)

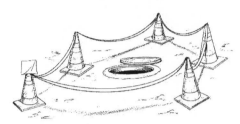

Coned-off area

Note: only if the above are considered as a raw construction material can they be turned into a Dungeon, eg, Ice Dungeons or Dungeon walls constructed from nets, etc.

Who are you and what history do you have with Dungeons?

Are you ready for more? Are you confident that you know enough facts about Dungeons? If so, it's time to figure out who you are and your relationship to the Dungeon in question.

It's no secret that medieval life was difficult. Most peasants spent half their life just trying to avoid being tossed into the Dungeon, spending the other half of their life working their way up through the feudal system.

Unlike most people who lived in the medieval times, you do not have to play this as a peasant.

You are creating this Dungeon now—but that does not mean you are the owner of the Dungeon. (We will explain the dynamics of this momentarily.)

So, who are you?

You will play as <u>one of these four character types</u>, each having their own particular way of interacting with Dungeons:

Dungeon Keeper

The boots on the ground of the Dungeon. A Dungeon keeper does all the hard work needed to keep the wheels greased and the prisoners screaming.

For smaller Dungeons, the Dungeon Keeper might do all the work, from the jailing to the torch-lighting to the safekeeping of treasures. As Dungeons scale up, Dungeon Keeper can evolve into a myriad of positions, often either overseeing or working alongside torturers, ticklers, jailers, miners, beast-tamers, beast-catchers, and sorcerers.

And who else but a flawed individual would voluntarily take to the depths of these Dungeons? You might become a Dungeon Keeper who spends all your time concerned with a very large pile of gold or a very rowdy crew of inmates.

Either way, it's important that you remember the bottom line over your own selfish ambitions: a Dungeon Keeper is the Keeper of the Dungeon.

Dungeon Prisoner

An occupant of a Dungeon, but not in a good way. Dungeon prisoners can take many forms—perhaps you're a political prisoner, a tortured enemy, or an insolvent serf. Depending on your approach, you can also play as a myriad of non-human Dungeon prisoners, including dragons, sasqui, goblins, or wolves.

Suffice it to say that, if you're a prisoner in a Dungeon, then something hasn't gone well for you in life.

Your main goal for being a Dungeon Prisoner is almost always to stop being a prisoner in a Dungeon, whether by escaping, earning a pardon, or politically maneuvering your way into joining the Dungeon Keeper's team.

Dungeon Explorer

This is the ultimate Dungeon outsider, literally. A Dungeon Explorer has no official association with the Dungeon, while also needing something from the Dungeon.

There are both noble and ignoble reasons to be a Dungeon Explorer. Perhaps you are there to rescue an old friend from the black cells, or perhaps for gold or the Holy Grail or a portal to another world.

Don't automatically assume Dungeon Explorers are honorable heroes. Like all four major Dungeon Characters, they almost always have something nefarious and shifty in their backstory. Otherwise, they'd be a normal Adventurer meandering amongst pyramids or through nature and waterfalls with little direction and certainly no gain. Hikers, if you will.

Something dangerous draws people to Dungeons. Think of some exciting motives, spooky backstories, and nefarious traits for your Dungeon Explorer.

Dungeon Lord

A person who owns a Dungeon. You want a Dungeon, but frankly have no time to design one or oversee its upkeep. That's fine: your Shadow Self is happy take this role over as its Dungeon Keeper.

A lord is the biggest deal in his or her particular jurisdiction, the man writing the checks so that everyone in the Dungeon is fed and starved at the appropriate levels, that the torch lamps will stay alit (without doing any of the lighting yourself), and that no one dies in the Dungeon, except for all the specific situations which someone needs to die.

Being a Dungeon Lord is not too different than a contemporary President of the United States, School District Superintendent, or CEO of a private prison. You're doing the tough work but often disconnected from the day-to-day grind... right up until things go off-the-rails and you're forced to jump in.

Obviously, the Dungeon Lord is also the character-type who spends the least amount of time in Dungeons. Unless you have a penchant for micro-management.

So, Which Dungeon Person Are You?

By now, you've probably decided which one you'll be. It's up to you to craft a realistic persona for your character—but don't go too far yet. We have a few more aspects of your character to iron out before you hop in!

Prisoners and Explorers

The prisoners line the walls. They look as if they've been here for ages, their beards thick, their garments rags, their eyes tired and unseeing.

"I'm Aelon and I'm here to save you from the terrible enemy who has trapped you here!" the hero announces.

"We do not deserve to be saved," they whisper.

"You should not be here," a voice says from behind Aelon. She whirls around to see a giant knight, surely eight feet tall, holding a gold sword. "I am the keeper of this Dungeon and you are not welcome here."

"I thought all keepers of Dungeons were ghouls and freaks." says the heroic Aelon.

"Then it seems you still have a far too limited perspective on a nuanced situation." says the Dungeon Keeper.

ADDITIONAL QUESTIONS AND DETAILS ABOUT YOUR DUNGEON LIFE

WHAT ARE YOUR DAILY TASKS LIKE?

Within the confines of this game, the Dungeon looms above all. The Lord worries about enemies and payments. The Keeper worries about much the same, but from a different angle. The Prisoner knows

A Dungeon Prisoner with little to do

nothing beyond this Dungeon, worried it may be where his or her journey ends. The Explorer once knew other things before plunging into the belly of this underground beast.

What do you do on a daily basis? What minutiae consume your life? If a Dungeon Keeper, it ranges from the Dungeon's mood curation to the feeding of the prisoners. If the Lord, you may be consumed more with making lists of enemies and determining how to get them into your Dungeon.

An Explorer probably had a journey to get to the Dungeon and now journeys within. A Prisoner doesn't have much control over daily life, but you have to imagine it nonetheless.

51

When did the Dungeon become the most important aspect of your character's life?

You were once an ordinary person. You had hopes and dreams before this place. Perhaps it was a sudden shift or perhaps you gradually went from one life to another, the Dungeon slowly consuming your waking life and your dreams.

Unless you were a child born in this Dungeon—which perhaps you were, and then you must sculpt a life story around that fact.

How did you hear about this Dungeon, or what event inspired you to create it? What is at stake if you aren't able to fulfill your duty as Dungeon Keeper?

Or, for what crimes were you imprisoned here?

Ask yourself: for how long has this been the world I know?

What did you do before the Dungeon began consuming your life?

Remember when you had a normal job? What was it? Bee keeper? Peasant? Non-Dungeon Lord?

How many Dungeons have you been in before this one? How does this compare?

Are you a Dungeon connoisseur or is this new for you? Have you visited one Dungeon or thousands? What were they like and how does this one differ?

It's good to know these questions, as they'll inform your behavior during your time in the Dungeons.

How do you generally feel about Dungeons?

Are they places you enjoy? Or are they unpleasant for you?

If you were locked in a Dungeon cell with a group of strangers, how long before you turn to murder and cannibalism to keep yourself alive?

This is always an important question, both in this game and any other you may play.

WHAT WAS THE FIRST DUNGEON YOU VISITED AND HOW DID IT INFORM THE REST OF YOUR LIFE MOVING FORWARD?

As we asked before, what is your history with Dungeons? But, specifically, recall the Dungeon you visited as a child or that, perhaps, you were born into. Recall the black mold on the sleek stones, the rattling chains, the wind howling down from the towers above and the other winds howling up from some deep chasm below the corridors through which you walked.

You still carry that Dungeon with you, today. You will carry that Dungeon with you always.

Enter the Shadow Self

It's time to start adding in some details to the Dungeon itself.

If you want this game to go well, you need to know the facts of the Dungeon.

"But," you might say, "how can I know these facts if I'm the Dungeon Explorer? Is it not unfair for me to have such information? Or, if I'm the Dungeon Lord, why am I concerned with such details? I want a Dungeon and don't bog me down with details! Or what has made me such an informed Dungeon Prisoner?"

Good questions, all of those—at least until you consider how wrong those questions are. These questions must be answered. How else will you play the game? The trouble is that, yes, for you to know the answers will complicate things. It will strip away mystery and intrigue and add a confused layer of grime over the entirety of the tale.

So you must play correctly.

NO LONGER A SILLY GAME

While we do have some important facts to figure out, it's crucial that you put your Shadow Self to better use in this game than you ever have before.

You may recall a game I taught you, once, ages ago. A game where you face off against a small sliver of yourself. Where you face your own shadow and hide something from it.

You've done things like this throughout the other games you've played, of course, but for this game you must do it again and on a higher level:

If you are to play as the *Explorer or Prisoner,*

then your Shadow Self must be *the Keeper and the Lord.*

If you are the *Lord or Keeper,*

then the Shadow Self plays as *the Explorer and the Prisoner.*

This is how it goes: draw upon the realms that exist within yourself to play this frightening game.

Crafting a Dungeon Experience

Now that we've gotten that out of the way, we have to determine some facts about the Dungeon.

WHAT KIND OF DUNGEON IS IT?

A Dungeon with little to offer

Seriously, what's the endgame for this thing? Just a place to keep prisoners? A place to torture prisoners? To kill them? A place to keep a terrible beast? A place to hide treasures? A place to even the score with that one demon?

Get the best idea of this you can. What is its purpose today, what was its purpose originally, and where is it headed?

Note: Upon answering this question, you may wish to scrap your previous conception of your Dungeon and start anew.

WHAT'S THE MOOD LIKE?

While Dungeons skew dreary, it's important to get the most crisp and clear idea of the mood that you can. Really close your eyes and reach a thorough envisioning of the exact experience of being in this Dungeon. Sounds. Smells. Sights.

Do you want distant wails of despair echoing through the corridors from prisoners, or will the subtle moaning of lost spirits suffice? A quiet resting place for the dead, or bustling with day-to-day traffic of chained prisoners? Will your cages rest on the ground, or will they sway in the air?

Ideally, this mood will send a strong message saying *watch out* to anyone who dares enter it.

WHERE IS MY DUNGEON?

Visualize the general political climate and geography in the area around it. Are you in Germany? Prussia? Some foreign land that never existed? A fantasy world in another realm? Peru? Quebec?

WHEN IS THE DUNGEON?

Sure, this game could have a medieval theme but it does not have to be in the true medieval times. Sure, Dungeons peaked during the middle ages, but their charm is timeless.

Is it five thousand years ago? Ten thousand? Two hundred? Is this a tale of the Byzantine Dungeons of 1066 or the Dungeons of the French revolution? The futuristic Dungeons of a derelict prison vessel floating through space?

WHAT TREASURES ARE HIDDEN IN THE DUNGEON? WHAT GHOSTS HAUNT IT? WHAT GHOULS WALK THE HALLS?

Always fun questions to answer!

Choosing a Dungeon Scenario

It's not easy being a Warrior. And here, at the end of her life, it seems that Aelon has ended up in chains and is doomed to die. She reaches for her food, beyond her grasp once again. She used to hear the screams of the other prisoners but not anymore. Perhaps there is no one left in this Dungeon, not even its frightening Keeper.

But then! Aha! She remembers hearing that this Dungeon contains a ghost who grants wishes to the dying. If only she can get close enough to death that she can make the wish....

"I've arrived, Aelon," says the Princess Ghost of the Forbidden Dungeon. "Now, sister, tell me your wish."

And so you now have the tools at your disposal in which you will create an enthralling Dungeon experience. There are two major baselines, both of which we have established by now, that you must cling to as you play this game. Beyond that, things are pretty flexible.

To reiterate:

- There must be a Dungeon, which you have conceived as either yourself or your Shadow Self
- You must have a connection to the Dungeon, either as its Lord, Keeper, Prisoner, or Explorer

Now, we ask the most important question:

Are you capable of conceiving and constructing a sprawling Dungeon, memorizing each and every corner and trap and also the greater world with each rhyme and reason for which it exists, all within the confines of your mind and memory?

No, while disappointing, is still an answer that I have accounted for. Since you are unable to conceive of a scenario in which your Dungeon is built, consider utilizing one of the scenarios that I have concocted and can vouch for as intelligent, thoughtful, inspiring premises for your first Dungeon adventure.

RELIGIOUS-THEMED SCENARIOS

- The Holy Grail is in the Dungeon
- A Demon Asked To Keep A Prisoner in the Dungeon Momentarily
- A Really Bad Guy is Escaping from the Dungeon (Religious)
- A Dragon Died in the Dungeon

MONSTER-THEMED SCENARIOS

- A Really Bad Guy is Escaping from the Dungeon (Monster Guy)
- A Monster Mix-Up At The Dungeon
- Who Let the Monsters Out?

LOGISTICS-THEMED SCENARIOS

- Too Many Slaves
- A Really Bad Guy is Escaping from the Dungeon (Political Prisoner)
- The Dungeon Includes a Portal to Hell that Must Be Sealed Off
- The Dungeon Employees Have Unionized And Are Striking
- We Ran Out Of Slaves
- A New Torture Chamber is Being Added And the Funding Fell Through
- Development Hell in Hell
- We Need A New Wing of the Dungeon
- A Visit From the Fire Marshall

GHOST-THEMED SCENARIOS

- The Dungeon is Being Used to Store Stolen Art and the Art is Haunted
- Who's Moaning?

SCENARIOS INSPIRED BY LITERATURE

- Dracula Owns the Dungeon
- Victor Frankenstein Works in the Dungeon
- A Really Bad Guy is Escaping from the Dungeon (Frankenstein's Monster)
- Wizard Boy and the Tower of London

SCENARIOS INSPIRED BY TRUE EVENTS

- Exploring the Catacombs of Paris.
- King Tut's Treasure is MINE! (See: ADVENTURE)
- Политический заключенный: A Gulag Story
- A Really Bad Guy is Escaping from the Dungeon (Prison Break)
- My Neighbor is Acting Suspicious

Did you choose? Are you ready?

A Journey Into Deep

YOU ARE NOW READY. THE TOOLS ARE AT YOUR DISPOSAL.

You have finally learned what a Dungeon is, what it isn't, and how to truly bring this Dungeon to life. Conceive your role, your scenario, and then finally, construct your Dungeon. Your Shadow Self is ready to go, already plotting surprises for you at the other end of everything.

This is my signature game. Perhaps not my only signature game, but something I want my enthusiasts to think of whenever they remember me. (Particularly after my death).

Enjoy.

Sincerely,

J. Theophrastus Bartholomew

GO!

TRUCKS

"HONK, HONK!"

Your air horn sends a deafening wave of sound through the crowd of children. They scream and cover their ears, running from the sidewalks, scared and searching for cover. A sly grin crosses your face, because they signaled you with the motion—the 'tugging at the air' motion —to honk your horn. They requested it without knowing what they were in for. You chuckle again: upgrading to an extra-loud horn for your big rig was worth every last penny!

This is just one of the many exciting encounters you'll have today on the road to Oklahoma City. You press down on the gas pedal, propelling your 80,000 pounds of steel across the American landscape. All eighteen wheels hug the tarmac as the road turns into a jet stream of black and yellow. There's no stopping you!

Become a legendary Truck driver by transporting goods around the greater United States of America. Buy low, sell high, upgrade your Truck, all while supporting yourself and your family. Choose the best routes! Encounter exciting situations! Do you have what it takes to deliver all your cargo and still get home in time for Christmas?

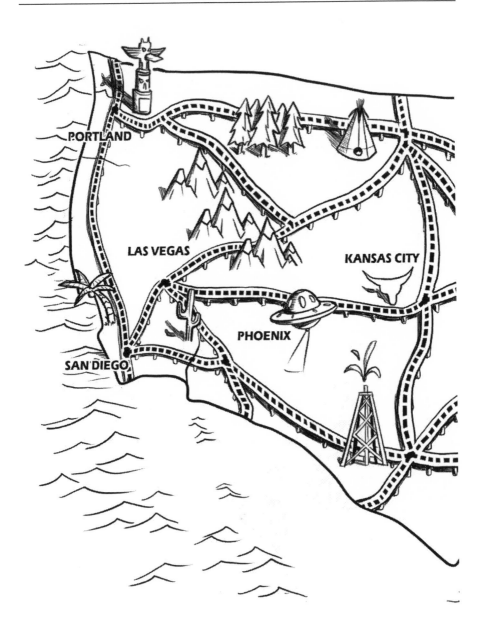

PORTLAND

LAS VEGAS

KANSAS CITY

PHOENIX

SAN DIEGO

LAND OF THE FREE,

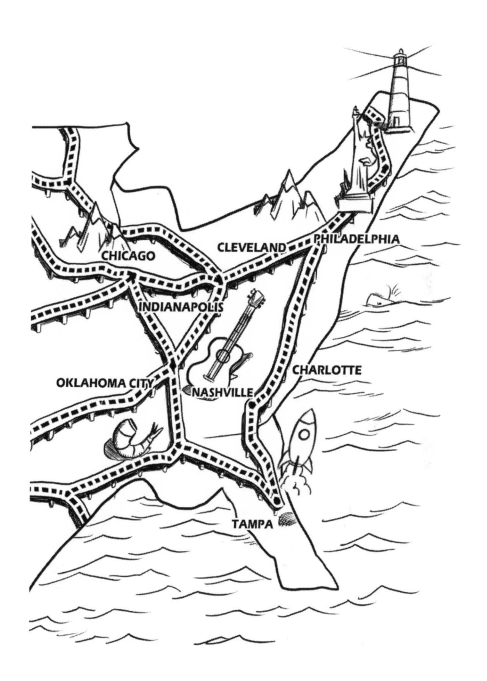

HOME OF THE BRAVE.

That was a map of the cities of this great nation, and the trade routes between them. Study this map carefully, then start by choosing a Hometown. Your Hometown is an important location that you may have to return to often. Take as much time as you need with this decision, because once you've selected a hometown, it CANNOT BE CHANGED.

- Nashville
- Indianapolis
- Charlotte
- Chicago
- Tampa
- Kansas City
- Philadelphia
- St. Louis
- Cleveland
- Phoenix
- Portland
- Oklahoma City
- Las Vegas

Have you chosen a Hometown? **Great.**

In Trucks, there are many ways to earn income, but the most common is buying and selling goods from one city to the next. Each city has unique goods that can be sold at a higher or lower cost, depending on demand. For a complete listing of cities and their goods, see the Economic Table.

Your Hometown, as it exists today

Brandt Bros. Regional Transport

A modest car pulls up to a business park inside your Hometown. The brick buildings are worn down and faded. One can tell that it's been years since any real business has been done here.

The car passes between a loose collection of warehouses before reaching a parking spot in front of building with a sign declaring *Brandt Bros. Regional Transport*. The sign is made of a flimsy plastic, the kind you'd see illuminated from behind at night. Each letter of it is outlined and accented with the company's trademark colors: orange and gold. The sign's aesthetics seem strangely familiar.

The car door opens, and someone steps out and walks through the door beneath the sign. That someone is you.

Brandt Bros. Regional Transport isn't just any *Trucking* and shipping business; it's one that's been in your family for years. Handed down from one generation to the next, it's the lifeblood of your family...

And today, it's in dire need of saving.

OLD SLY WILLY

Small bells attached to the door ring as you enter a dim mechanic's office. A man sits at a table filled with papers, lit only by a crooked hanging fluorescent bulb. He turns to greet you.

"So you finally decided to step up to the plate?" The man says, looking you over. "Take over the family business? Trucking ain't never an easy job, but someone's gotta do it. Good to see you."

"*Willy*" reads the embroidered patch on his stained work shirt, just below a pack of cigarettes in his shirt pocket. He's the human equivalent of what you'd imagine a stale piece of bread crust to be like: stale, crusty, and world weary. The left half of his face is withered and leathery from the years of sitting in the driver's seat under direct sunlight, a telltale sign that this man knows his Trucks. After his years of service, Willy now resides in this office.

But why introduce this character?

What effect is he to have on your game of Trucks?

Well, this meager man is your uncle. He has been diligently maintaining the business for years, through thick and thin.

"As you know," he continues with age and gravel in his voice, "the company's great Trucking fleet has all but whittled away because of the hard times. It's a shadow of its former glory, but I'm keeping my head up. Why? Well, your father left one last Truck just for you, and with it, I think you might have a shot at turning things around. Ah, your old pops always knew you'd come back."

Under your guidance, Old Sly Willy will act as the book keeper of the business. He will process and handle payments, receipts, and will always give you free repairs on your vehicles.

Old Sly Willy shuffles over to an empty rack of key hooks. The rack is empty except for one glimmering pair of keys, which he takes off and tosses to you. "Your father's Truck. It's not much kid, but it's enough to get us on our feet again."

He motions towards the garage, where you see a beige 1981 Ford F150, with a little rust eating away underneath the paint.

"It's not a looker," he says, "but with the size of that bed, I reckon you'll be able to fit two pallets of goods in there. Now now, before you start asking where the big Trucks are, let me just say one thing: Big Trucking starts with little Trucks, just how your father started this business in the first place. You've gotta work your way up, and now, we're counting on you."

Pause for a moment to consider how you'd like to respond to such a momentous statement from Old Sly Willy.

But wait, before you can, he continues:

"Say," he says, arching an eyebrow and sizing you up and down. "How've you been all these years? And how's your family?"

I'VE GOT A TRUCK - NOW WHAT?

Your first Truck, which came at no cost, is loaded with two pallets of CORN. It's your goal to sell this corn for a profit, which in turn you will use to buy more items, support your family, and maintain your livelihood. Take a look at the map and consult the Economic Table for locations on where to sell. I recommend selling where the demand is highest, and then using those funds to buy items priced at below-average prices. This is the fundamental money-making system in the Game of Trucks.

Once you're all set, you'll hop in your Truck, crank those keys, travel the country, and make a name for yourself as a Trucking legend.

Your Hometown Family

Wait a second, mister! Where do you think you're headed in the Truck? This is a FAMILY business! Before you hit the road, you have to build a realistic family. Envision what kind of family you would like, although remember that you have to keep it realistically within your annual salary.

A few things to consider.

- Are you married, single, divorced, or separated?
- How many children do you have? You must have as few as two or as many as nine.
- What are your children named? What are their favorite subjects in school?
- Which child is your favorite? Which is your least favorite? Rank the children in order of preference, including the least positive traits of each child.
- Do you live in an apartment, a house, a trailer, or townhome?
- How many cats do you have? You can have as few as four or as many as fifteen.
- How many dogs do you have? Also, on a scale of 1 to 10, rate their level of ferality.

This family is located in your Hometown, and permanently resides there. They cannot move away from this city under any circumstances.

Got the family figured out?

Get ready, because I'll tell you something right now: *you don't know the half of it.*

More Trucks

IN THE GAME OF TRUCKS, THERE ARE PLENTY OF TRUCKS.

As you progress through the game, you'll have opportunities at Truck stops to trade and upgrade your Truck to bigger and better models. Each Truck has unique qualities to it, all fitted for different transport situations.

Ford F150 - Range: 200 miles. Wheels: 4. Capacity: 2 Pallets. (Free)

Rented Van - Range: 300 miles. Wheels: 6. Capacity: 4 Pallets. ($10/day)

Van

Box Truck (Medium) - Range: 200 miles. Wheels: 6. Capacity: 8 Pallets. ($7,000)

Box Truck (Large) - Range: 250 miles. Wheels: 6. Capacity: 12 Pallets. ($10,000)

Flatbed Truck - Range: 300 miles. Wheels: 6. Capacity: 8 Pallets, expandable to 14. ($9,000)

Dump Truck - Range: 100 miles. Wheels: 6. Capacity: 48000 pounds of loose items. ($18,000)

Semi-Trailer

Semi-Trailer Truck - Range: 1300 miles. Wheels: 18. Capacity: 42 Pallets. ($24,000)

Semi-Trailer Truck (Double) - Range: 700 miles. Wheels: 24. Capacity: 84 Pallets. ($32,000)

Monster Truck - Range: 50 miles. Wheels: 4. Capacity: 1 Pallet. ($45,000)

Upgrades:

Horn: Loud, Extra Loud, Illegal Loud

Wheels: Big, Extra Big, Super Big with Spikes

Seats: Cloth, Leather

Sound system: Radio, Cassette, CD

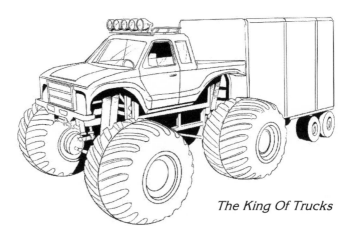
The King Of Trucks

Additional Communications: Short-Range radio, Long-Range radio, Portable Cellular Car Phone, J.E.F.F. Navigation Computer

Driving Your Truck

Through a rabble of poplars and spruce comes the beast you've been fearing: a 10% grade down the slopes of Idaho. You hit the shift

stick and pop into eighth. The engine whines, the cab jolts, and you watch your RPMs shoot through the roof.

Suddenly, two 4-Wheelers take jabs at your cab, but you're able to dodge them.

40. 41. 42.

The speed creeps up on you like a strangling serial killer.

43. 44. 45.

You look in your mirror and a whole swarm of 4-Wheelers approaches. That leaves you no choice. You could flip on your Maxis and maintain a safe speed, but with that many on your tail, you take your chances.

With white knuckles you barrel down that hill!

Driving a Truck might seem easy, but here are the types of obstacles you will encounter on the road:

A Strong Truck being attacked by a 4-Wheeler

HILLS

Trucks can get very big and very heavy, so it's important to stay in control when going down hills. Use your gearing to control your speed rather than your brakes, as your brakes are prone to starting on fire and exploding because of the massive amount of pressure and friction. If you lose control of your speed, you are prone to accidents, or in extreme circumstances, Jack Knifing, a phenomenon where the weight of your trailer takes over, pushing the cab at a 120° angle as you barrel down a hill to your death.

4-Wheelers

The bane of all truckers, 4-Wheelers are any vehicle on the road that's NOT A TRUCK. At any time, kamikaze swarms of 4-Wheelers will surround your Truck and attempt to knock you from the road. They will cut you off, try to sneak in next to you while turning. Sometimes, they'll even come at you directly, ready to kill.

What they don't know is that their small size and weight makes them effectively harmless against you, so the real threat comes when you lose control attempting to avoid them. As long as you maintain a constant speed, you should be able to plow right through them.

2-Leggers

Pedestrians come in all shapes and sizes, and rarely will you see them on the highway. The concussive blast of an extra-loud air horn will knock most away from the road.

Again, relatively harmless to your vehicle, unless you lose control attempting to avoid them.

Car Jackers

As rising crime sweeps the nation, a more aggressive and highly armed splinter group of 2-Leggers will actively try and steal the goods from your Truck. Armed with Uzis, they create barricades between coveted trading posts and truck stops.

Some will try and slow your Truck by pretending to ask for help or directions, others will commandeer 4-Wheelers and attempt to take you out while on the road in a moving convoy. Some will simply open fire with their Uzis when they see you approaching.

Outfitting your Truck with barbed wire to prevent Car Jackers from jumping onto your truck may help. Replacing your lug nuts with sharp, pointed spikes will also help against hostile 4-Wheelers.

If Car Jackers persist, visit any Truck Stop to purchase a sawed-off shotgun, or any other firearm that can be operated while you have one hand on the wheel.

Truck Stops

Your air brakes hiss as you step out of the cab. Your two snakeskin cowboy boots hit the wet black top. It's night time at the Truck Stop, and you need to rest these boots. The Truck Stop lights up the darkness, and from the diner within you see a warm light. Looks safe, right?

At a booth, you order a juicy burger and fries. Tabasco on the side, please. You like your fries with a little kick. But right before you bite into this delicious feast, you hear someone call your name!

Two-Time Tony and his crew want a word with you. Apparently, you've been running Trucks on their turf, and now they want a cut. You've got a six shooter in your pocket and a knife in your other pocket.

Talk it out? Or take 'em out?

In every city is a Truck Stop. They provide rest, recuperation, opportunities for socializing, and they act as trading hubs for their area.

Here's what you can expect to find in your average truck stop:

Fuel Station - Refuel your truck and get ready for the next leg.

Rest Stop - Warm beds and clean sheets, open 24 hours. Get some sleep!

Diner - Tummy rumbling? Fill up the tank in your body with some juicy bacon and eggs!

Trading Post - Interface with local economies and sell your wares. Check out those cool wraparound sunglasses, too! Only $3.99, what a deal! You deserve a cool nickname like "Sting Ray" or "Chop Dog" with a pair of wraparound shades that cool.

Garage - Truck too slow? Need bigger horns? Upgrade and repair your vehicle here.

Brothel - Life on the road is lonely, and you can find some temporary companionship here in the form of male and female companions.

Note: At this point in constructing your game world, it's no surprise that you're missing your family right about now. You've been away for months, and they're so far away. You've even considered bringing them with you on the road, but you know that won't work. The rules dictate that they must PERMANENTLY reside in your Hometown!

Your Other Family

Remember when we decided that you had to choose your family? Of course you do—that happened moments ago.

Well, we've got some news for you: regardless of what you chose, you have a family in another state, too. That's right: you're one of *those* Truckers.

Creating a second family while on the road is an inevitability of Truck life and an efficient solution to the solitude you endure. When one family disappears into the horizon, another one rises in front of you, closer and closer with every mile.

It's best that your second family has considerable distance from your Hometown family. Coastal splits are the obvious choice for some, but there are other methods.

Is there a city from your travels that you keep coming back to, perhaps one you enjoy more than your Hometown? Consider choosing that city to start your second family.

To make it easier, feel free to find a partner with the same name, and consider re-using the names of the children of one family for the other.

Family Life, Road Life

Work/life balance is always a difficult task for most. Careers can lead to fulfillment, both emotionally and financially, but sometimes they get in the way. This is especially difficult for Truckers like you—months spent away, on the road, nomadically venturing forth as your family (or families) anxiously await your return.

Ultimately, a strong family life leads to a strong road life, so to spice things up while on the road you'll get to solve a few of these challenging family scenarios. They could happen at any moment, so watch out!

MOMMY'S PREGNANT

Difficulty level: Medium

This event occurs when you have not returned to your Hometown for 3-9 months.

The road looks all clear, sunlight gleaming off the desert highway. Suddenly, your car phone rings. Caller ID has your name on it. What could it be? You answer the phone and it's your youngest child.

"Mommy's pregnant again! I don't want another little brother!" the children cry.

But the math doesn't add up, you think. How could she be pregnant if you haven't been home for 3-9 months?

From the moment you get this phone call, you'll now have only 0-6 months at the most to finish up your outstanding jobs and travel back to your Hometown to investigate the matter.

WHAT HAPPENED TO OLD SLY WILLY?

Difficulty level: Traumatic

This event occurs if your profit margin drops to 5% or less for three months.

Cigarette smoke hangs in the office of Brandt Bros. Regional Transport, where Old Sly Willy sits crunching the numbers. They aren't what they used to be, and margins are slim these days. He can barely afford to keep the lights on.

An exhausted expression takes over his face. He's lived a long, tough life, and the hard times haven't made it any easier. He sets down his pen and he closes his eyes, if only for a moment.

A single tear falls from his eye, and splashing onto the tip of his cigarette, extinguishing it. And with no better metaphor to signal his death, Old Sly Willy passes away on the spot. He had a good run.

With Old Sly Willy out of the picture, it's time to outfit the office with new employees. Head back home and choose from any member of your Hometown family for this job.

LITTLE LLOYD WANTS TO GO TO DISNEY WORLD

Difficulty level: Catastrophic.

This event occurs if you are married in both of your families.

Also, this one really gets the nerves racing. Not for the faint of heart.

Commonly a child will express their interest in going to Disney World during the winter holidays. Now, this can be a wonderful experience for the man with one family, but for the man with two: *woah boy*, this one is going to be a headache.

A random child from each of your families has convinced their respective mother that going to Disney World will be a good idea, and in turn, has convinced you. Don't try and stop them: they've already all purchased the tickets. How do you handle this?

Both families will have rented rooms at opposite ends of the Walt Disney World Resort for a fun filled holiday trip. The days will likely overlap, but not completely.

Here is an encounter you will need to cover up:

You've just hopped off the Indiana Jones ride, and they're printing photos of everyone's horrified expressions during the animatronic snake scare, taken from an automated camera. However, you spot your Hometown family exiting the ride as well, so you keep your head low because you said you wouldn't show up for another two days. Then it gets worse. Lloyd, one of your Hometown children, and your least favorite of them all, pipes up.

"That man looks like daddy!" He's right. Apparently, the automated photo captured some damning evidence suggesting that you and your Other Family were riding in the cart behind them, the whole ride.

Do you turn around and admit you've arrived early, or do you continue exiting with Family B, biding your time in hopes that this will all blow over?

Keep in mind that if the two families come into contact physically with each other at ANY point during this trip, or ever, even if you're not present, the marriages on both sides will immediately dissolve.

Naturally, all of this will have a disastrous effect on your psyche.

Note: If your family disintegrates and you've undergone the What Happened To Old Sly Willy scenario, your office will be vacant and all business transactions instantly come to a halt, as no family will be left to work there.

Economic Table

Cities are famous, and it's easy to see why: they've all got unique items that make them memorable.

Here is a table with the items you will be able to buy and trade between cities, and their current market value at the start of the game.

Note: Once the game begins, market value will begin to fluctuate depending on a variety of in-game circumstances which you will have to calculate.

CITY	KNOWN FOR	SELL PRICE	NEEDS	BUY PRICE
Nashville	Whiskey	$10	Tobacco	$3
	Guitars	$42	Meat	$34
Indianapolis	Coal	$16	Wheat	$2
	Engines	$100	Steel	$30
Charlotte	Tobacco	$1	Sand	$1
	Planes	$8000	Lumber	$13
Chicago	Corn	$3	Gypsum	$230
	Hot Dogs	$5	Playing Cards	$66
Tampa	Fish	$6	Electricity	$23
	Limes	$7	Engines	$450
Kansas City	Meat	$23	Guitars	$78
	Gypsum	$99	Oil	$11
Philadelphia	Steel	$24	Oil	$7
	Coal	$21	Soybeans	$2
St. Louis	Meat	$35	Lumber	$18
	Soybeans	$1	Whiskey	$48
Toledo	Corn	$2	Coal	$29
	Waste	$.39	Steel	$47
Phoenix	Sand	$.32	Fish	$12
	Waste	$.35	Hot Dogs	$19
Portland	Lumber	$4	Corn	$7
	Electricity	$14	Planes	$12500
Oklahoma City	Oil	$3	Waste	$.97
	Wheat	$.76	Limes	$12
Las Vegas	Playing Cards	$53	Coal	$39
	Sand	$.69	Whiskey	$87

Hitting The Road

The leather interior squeaks as you hop inside, and the steel door of your Father's F150 slams shut as you close it, rattling the cab. You kick the empty old cans of Hamm's Beer away from the pedals.

'Ha', you think, 'Pops sure loved his beer.' The keys fit into the ignition like a glove.

Vroom! The engine starts with a cough and a kick.

So you've figured it all out. You've got your truck, your family, your business is all in order, and you've finally chosen your first destination. That means it's time to hit the road. Here are some final tips on having a great Trucks experience:

- Choose optimal routes to maximize efficiency. Instead of listing all the possible routes in this book, we recommend that you take some time to sit down with an atlas and familiarize yourself with every major interstate in the country.
- Avoid bad traffic and road construction.
- Drive without any accidents. A collision will slow you down!
- Don't let thieves or carjackers hold up your Truck.
- Consider what you will do to occupy your mind while on the road. Consider playing one of the other games in this book within Trucks, as otherwise Trucks could get boring!

You check the fuel: full.

You adjust the mirrors.

Your two pallets of CORN? Secured tightly.

Your boot hovers over the pedal.

Are you ready to hit the road?

GO!

THE VISITOR

"WHAT HAPPENED TO THE BACKYARD?" YOUR MOTHER SHOUTS,

"It looks as if someone has been digging up holes. _____, did you do this?"

"I did not, Mother," you say. "It must have been the neighbors again. I think they got a new dog."

"This was not the work of a dog! This is the work of something different. Did you make someone at school mad at you?"

Of course, you cannot admit it, but you know who and what dug up the backyard. You had a hand in it. The answer is beyond your Mother's comprehension and stretches back across the galaxy to a small moon known as Uhlvidia--and the visitors who came from there and landed on Earth.

Smalltown, Minnesota. 1982. The fabric of your quiet childhood existence is torn to shreds when a creature appears in your backyard and creates a ripple of circumstances that will send you on a dark quest unlike anything you've ever imagined.

Sometimes the greatest action one can take is that of inaction. Sometimes saving the galaxy as we know it requires no response at all, if presented the right opportunity.

In this story, you will be tested.

Good luck on saving the universe, kid.

One: The Mining Town

Yours is a mining town, there in the windswept northern land they call the Range of Iron. The land is pockmarked and ravaged, torn to pieces and shreds by the ranks of thoughtless men who attack the ground and bleed it dry of all it holds. Cogs in the machine of big business, hard-hatted and steel-toed vampires who march across the land with the goal to only destroy it.

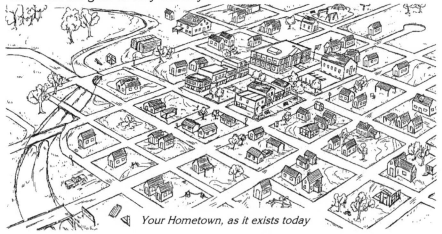

Your Hometown, as it exists today

Your school bus crosses these lands—hot and humid and swarming with flies and bugs in the hot days like today. During the other half of the year, snowdrifts and cold terror embrace the land.

You sit alone on the bus once again. You're five reading levels above these classmates, these cretins and stooges with little to say and nothing to add to your life. Not that the teachers understand you: sixth grade can be such a grind. Men and women looming over you, telling you where to go and what to do. What to think. Who to be.

At home, your father remains absent, your siblings slugs, your mother serving you a frozen dinner that you eat in front of the television in the air conditioned box these people call a home.

As a child, consider this question: What do you want to be when you grow up?

Two: Night

And now you are reading your comic book inside the tent in which you sleep. The tent that serves as a backyard bedroom every warm-enough evening. The light of your flashlight illuminates visions of superheroes and villains on weathered paper pages. You've read this tale a thousand times but it does not grow old, not this Adventure.

You love these moments, these brief times of the day that you can own yourself.

Until a voice interrupts everything.

"Excuse me, sir," *peeps a growling, whispering voice from outside your tent.* "Can you spare some water?"

A new character is about to join this story. A character that will change your life forever. You will have two options, consider them wisely:

1. Shine your light outside the tent, into the darkness.
2. Stay inside and pretend you did not hear anything.

If you choose the second option, let's be clear that this game is not for you. Forget it all and skip ahead to **Step Thirteen**—or, more realistically, if you can't handle shining your light from the tent out into the darkness then you should probably just walk away from this book of games altogether. And skip the library. You're not up to the task, bub.

Assuming that you choose to shine your light into the darkness (and not simply put down this book), here is what you will see: a small figure crouched against the fence.

"Before I step out from the darkness," *it says*, "you must know that I'm not of your world. Please do not shout or scream or attack me when you see what I look like. For I am a frightening creature to those who have not seen the likes of me before."

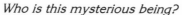

Imagine what a creature from outside our world might look like. He could be short, he could be tall, green or grey, well-spoken or slack-jawed. Let your imagination run wild with what this creature could look like. He clearly speaks English so that narrows the scope a little bit at least.

Who is this mysterious being?

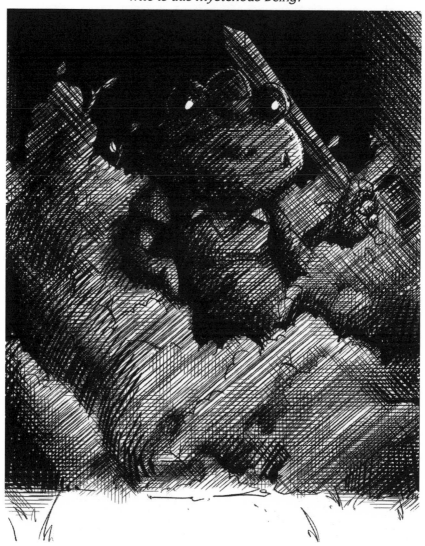

Got it?

Good. Turn the page once your imagination has solidified the appearance of this mysterious being.

The figure steps out further into the light and you get a better look at it.

    This is what the creature is revealed to look like. A small creature, about two feet tall, that looks like a smiling anthropomorphized toad with a paper route, but also holding a sword in its right hand. His clothes consist of navy-blue shorts, boat shoes, a white collared shirt and a schoolboy cap, and the sword is about two feet long and gleams in the light of your flashlight.

      "If you are reluctant to give me water," *the creature says,* "first, I will tell you my story."

Three: The Visitor's Tale

The following is what the creature tells you from its spot hidden along the fence:

"I am what they call a Uhlvidian Warrior-Toad. That is what I call myself, at least, to help you understand who it is that I am.

We Uhlvidians have a strict code of conduct and one of our most important rules is that we always politely ask for things. We never threaten or steal.

I'm a very thirsty creature who has had a long journey but I don't mind explaining some more things first. I suspect that you could share water with me. Your outpost in this grassy landscape, while not closely guarded, seems well stocked.

The wooden box-like fortress you guard looks well-fortified. If you could allow me entrance briefly, I would appreciate some sustenance. But I am no stranger to well-fortified fortresses. The kingdom of Uhlvidia is on a distant planet, a world of magic and conflict, of untamed and unknown landscapes.

I am called Drexxel. My people call ourselves the Toads, as I said.

Every Uhlvidian creature—all three thousand species that inhabit the planet, including the animals and amoebas and talking walking mushrooms—are under dire threat from an evil that invaded our planet from outside the atmosphere.

Giant robotic insects who call themselves the Viktorians. They intend to turn the planet into a new mine that they can use for taking the rich resources they've already stripped from their own world.

We've decided to seek other planets which are the next victims of the Viktorians. And Earth is at the top of their list. They intend to come here for all your resources before you can use them yourselves.

We need you to prepare yourselves for their invasion. And, if you're willing, you can bring your best soldiers back to Uhlvidia with me.

Now, I need a glass of water and then we have to plan our trip to the United Nations. Will you provide me with some water, please?"

Four: The Water

Note: Drexxel has but moments to live at this point.

Drexxel the Uhlvidian Warrior-Toad has asked you for a glass of water. However, he is from Outer Space and is certainly unfamiliar with the wide selection of beverages on Earth.

Because you're outside, a hose lies next to you, ready to spray at full blast at a moment's notice. Inside, there are cups and a faucet, which you can serve from. Also, inside your refrigerator lies *Orange Juice, Milk, a Twelve Pack of Hamm's Beer, a six pack of Diet Pepsi, and a two-liter bottle of Squirt who no one knows who opened.*

This information boils down to three options: either give him a glass of water, provide an alternative to water, or simply refuse his request.

Now that you understand what options are at your disposal, it's time to make a decision.

> *At a Glance: If he dies, his storyline is gone forever, but his body will provide scientists with years of questions to solve. If he lives, he will bring you along on an extraordinary journey.*

- If you refuse him water, he will die of dehydration within thirty seconds.
- If you give him water, it will poison him and he will die. (contaminated)
- If you give him an alternative, such as soda or iced-tea, he will ramble about his Home Planet on a euphoric sugar-high for 15 minutes and then die, abruptly.

All deaths will occur in front of you and will involve a seizure, some frothing at the mouth, and limbs kicking around as he breathes his last.

> *Note from the Editors: We were hesitant to include The Visitor in this book because of the glaring "bug" which results in no condition for success (saving Drexxel's life). However, the game is still playable (and still robust) upon his death. In good faith, here is the rest of the game as it stands.*

Five: The Body

You stand over Drexxel's non-responsive body, trying to remember everything you've ever learned in health class. How to revive a dead body. How to save someone on the precipice of death. But do these things work on a Warrior-Toad?

You've obeyed his commands, but now small Drexxel's body lies before you. Now what?

Players may attempt CPR or mouth-to-mouth on Drexxel's dead body. If you choose to perform one of these hopeless acts, take a moment to imagine what that experience would be like.

Keep in mind that Drexxel is dead and will continue to be dead. But, if it will make you more comfortable with this game as it progresses, you can attempt to revive him for as long as you'd like.

Once you've established that his death is certain—whether it takes you ten seconds or ten minutes—it's time to decide what to do with his body.

As a Child, your options for what to do with the body include:

➢ Try to bury it without pomp or ceremony in your yard.
➢ Go sleep in the bedroom you share with your brothers and pretend this whole thing never happened. Let someone else find the toad body.
➢ Plan a small funeral by yourself and bury it with some dignity, perhaps in the woods where you play.
➢ Confide in and present your findings to your Science Teacher in the morning.

Begin preparations for your decision.

Six: More Toads

This is a lot to handle for such a young kid like yourself!
But suddenly, you are interrupted...

"What happened here?" a voice in the darkness wails from behind you. You spin around and shine your flashlight into the other corner of the yard. You see a bare minimum of five more Toads standing there looking at you.

"Oh no!" wails one of them, an older one with a feminine quality to her voice. The five of them run and gather around the body, each trying to revive it, splashing water on its face and trying a similar form of CPR. Soon, they lose steam and begin poking it with sticks.

"Not Drexxel! What was he doing off the spaceship!? How did this happen?"

"We can't talk about this right here," says a different Toad, the largest of them, holding two battle axes. "Come with us, boy. Everyone, to the spaceship!"

More toads. Do they need beverages as well, or are we past that, now?

Seven: Decisions

At this moment, you have a new decision to make.

If you say **"no"** to following the Toads to their spaceship, you'll keep playing this game but the conflict will consist entirely of going to school and working to gradually enjoy your life better, despite having had a bizarre traumatizing experience in which you killed an alien in your backyard and then talked to his family before walking away and pretending it didn't happen. No other directions will be provided.

Are you refusing? If so, skip to **Step Thirteen**.

Then, that's that for you.

We dare you to say yes to this plan. Its boundless amphibious insanity is surely too much for a Child's mind like you own, so proceed at your own peril.

Eight: The Spaceship

The Toads introduce themselves and welcome you into the ship, a giant orb with lots of floating pods where Toads (and you) sit and stand. There is now a bare minimum of six of them, plus the dead Drexxel, who sits on a burlap sack in the middle of the ship, bringing the number technically up to seven.

Left to right, Burlish, Girlish, Chexxel, Rexxel, Madame Whirlish, Chadpole.

This is who they are:

- **Burlish:** The largest and toughest Warrior-Toad of them all. The apparent muscle and, at times, the loudest and most leaderful of the Toads.
- **Girlish:** A Lady-Warrior-Toad, tough and scowling but with some gentle feminine qualities mixed in.
- **Chexxel:** A Bard-Warrior-Toad, good at both fighting and singing.
- **Rexxel:** A Cleric-Toad. It appears that their names are not as closely aligned with their classes as you might have suspected. He's scholarly, it seems.
- **Madame Whirlish:** A Diviner-Toad. She seems to know a lot about magic spells and might be something of a priestess.
- **Chadpole:** In contrast to his name, Chadpole is actually a very dashing older Warrior-Toad and the skilled pilot of the spaceship.

Nine: Questions

After the introductions, all the Toads turn their focus to their individual stations on the bridge of this ship, leaving you to watch in silence. The ship takes off and begins exiting the atmosphere. It seems the adventure has begun.

Unsure what a child's role in all this will turn out to be, it's best to spur some conversation to fill the air.

I. **"Is there anything I can do?"** They may find a task for you.
II. **"Would you like help planning the funeral?"** If you ask this question, you can rest assured that they'll refuse without specific explanation or elaboration, but that you might have to explain to them that, as a sixth grader, your own knowledge regarding funeral planning is limited.

III.   "Have you guys been to Earth before?" Almost a guarantee
        that they won't have much to say in response to this.
IV.   "I heard about the Viktorians from Drexxel. Sounds pretty
        scary." Yeah, can't say that this would be a great move, but
        worth a shot, just to see if you can learn some more backstory.
V.   "Why do you think he died?" Highly not recommended. Imagine
        that they'll potentially blame you if you open this can of worms.
VI.   "What do you think of Michael Jackson?" Perhaps your
        introduction of contemporary music to them will strengthen some
        sort of cultural bond. If you have a cassette or vinyl record, you
        may wish to present it.
VII.   Any other idea you have.

After you hem and haw in your efforts to make small talk,
you realize that Madame Whirlish has been planning on speaking
first, and has been patiently waiting for you to finish.

Ten: Hell and Diplomacy

"We will not be planning a funeral," *she says.* "While his body
is still freshly deceased, we must rescue his soul from the afterlife and
initiate his ressurection. A funeral would be an acceptance of failure.
Drexxel was our precocious prodigy. The prophecy says so. Don't
worry, we do not hold you accountable for his death but we do need
your help."

Everyone agrees at this moment.

"We must abandon the material plane, cross the astral plane,
and descend into the eight realms of Uhlvidian Hell in order to find his
soul in one of the realms. It's important that you understand every
layer of the Uhlividian afterlife," *she says*, "So that we can find him."

Choose whether to say **yes** or **no** to indicate you understand. If
you choose **no**, imagine what it would be like if Madame Whirlish spent
longer explaining the Uhlividian concept of life after death and how it
more closely relates to Valhalla or the Grecian afterlife, rather than the
Dantean concept of hell being a place for the wicked and damned.

"It's also important that you understand how important
Drexxel was. He was—and still is—our hero to save us against the
Viktorians. He is a Warrior-Toad, yes, but he's also a very special kind
of toad: a Diplomat Toad. Yes, a diplomat. The most skilled and
graceful negotiator Uhlvidia has ever known. He is the middle child of
a family of four hundred and seventy three brothers and sisters. We
need his charm and his grace and his negotiating abilities if we are to

successfully negotiate a path through the galaxy and rally the other planets needed to defeat the Viktorians."

Eleven: The Eight Realms of Hell

"There are eight realms of Hell and we will scour each one for his soul." explains Madame Whirlish.

Limbohell: The most mild of the hells. A purgatorial, bland, milquetoast hell, where nothing much happens except the transfer of souls between the other hells. It's a pretty ordinary hell, all told, mostly populated by middle management and pencil pushers. Not much to complain about, either. Not one of the really bad ones.

Water Hell: A world of seas, with no dry land. The inhabitants are either those who loved water the most or hated it the most—making it both a nightmare and a paradise, depending on who visits it and who is trapped there. Some members of Water Hell spend their entire existence in the water drowning for all eternity, while others sail or canoe across its surface.

Valhella: The warrior hell. Where the warriors go for glory at the end of their battles and lives. Most of those who populate Valhella arrived there via death on the battlefield.

Knighthell: A lot like Valhella, but for the specific class of Warrior-Toads who've been knighted ceremoniously. The punished are doomed to eternal combat.

Summer Hell: A warm place of sandy beaches and clear-blue lakes and endless bicycle rides and no school for any children and barbeques on the lawn, although it can get a little hot. Sometimes terribly hot. And sometimes there's summer school, never-ending summer school for all the Scholar-Toads who never studied as hard as they should have.

Cloud Hell: A cool, breezy hell. It's nice unless you're terrified of heights. Lots of harps. Most are punished with eternal falling.

Nighthell: The place that's always dark, always night, always slightly colder than the day was, although in a world without day. For some

Night-Toads, this is a delightful place, full of possibility and wonder. For others, it's a place of fear and confusion and monsters under the Toadbed.

Normal Hell: Hell.

Each of these hells is filled with a bevy of mysterious tricksters and sinful occupants, so be weary of all you may encounter.

Twelve: Go to Hell

The Madame makes the mission clear for you:

Figure out which of those hells Drexxel is in and choose who will join you.

You might be wondering now why they are insistent on you joining. The answer is simple: they are more likely to succeed if they bring the person responsible for Drexxel's death.

You may choose two companions for this quest. At least one of them should be a member of the Toadship. The other one can only be chosen by you and it should be someone you know well.

Someone you know intimately but who does not know Drexxel. Think about everyone you know, everyone in your quiet life in this boring mining town. Of course, you can bring anyone you want. I have a strong recommendation on who should help for the journey into all the hells. Someone else who can always help.

One obvious choice is to choose your Science Teacher, the only adult in your life that you can confide in.

But let me recommend another companion... Close your eyes and conjure the shadow creature that walks alongside and throughout your prismed soul.

Your Shadow Self.

Your Shadow Self.

Your Shadow Self.

Your Shadow Self.

Your Shadow Self is naturally a hellwalker. Its translation skills and local knowledge will be necessary. It's time to go to darker worlds than you've ever known and you're going to need all the help you can get.

Now, with a Toad of your choice on one side and your Shadow Self on the other, it's time to go to Hell.

It's Time For Your Story To Begin

And so, with the help of the Uhlvidian collective, their Toadship, and the accompaniment of a companion, you venture forth on your mission. The mysteries of the universe unfold as your Toadship miraculously rockets towards the first hell of your choosing.

Who knows what may await. What are the hells like? What do these Uhlvidian people have to offer?

And yet to answer: what are Drexxel's *sins*? Do they weigh so heavy that he has earned eternal damnation? Or has he earned a place of peaceful prominence in one of the hells? These sins may provide you with clues as to which hell he's been sent to.

Perhaps this visitor was there for more than a visit...

GO!

Thirteen: It's all Over

Phew! Sigh of relief! It's finally time for school, once again. Everything is finally back to normal. No more aliens! Just good old fashioned real life. The bus picks you up and you're on your way...

Inside the halls of your school, no one notices that you just underwent an alien encounter. Charlie sticks his tongue out at you. Benny shoves you aside, for no reason. Lily makes eye contact with you for a suspicious amount of time. Likely an accident.

Regardless, none of them know of the encounter you had last night. And if you don't speak up, no one will...

...until...

Science class is first on your schedule, naturally. Your Science Teacher has a full class of learning prepared, you can tell.

But he bites his lip. Something is wrong. Before the bell strikes 8:00, he comes to you desk to deliver a message. "I'm sorry, but you're needed at the principal's office."

Gulp.

And in the principal's office...

The police chief and a sergeant are waiting for you. They sit you down in a chair, and give you a small glass of water and a choice of any snack from the vending machine. They're about to deliver a very shocking message to you, and want you to be comfortable.

The police chief solemnly takes off his hat and tells you the reason for why you've been called here.

He'll deliver one of these two messages, depending on the choices you have made:

I.   A dehydrated alien has been found in your backyard, and your mother is coming to pick you up immediately as you are now moving from your childhood home forever.

II. Your father got into a Trucking accident out of state and it has been revealed that he has been living a double life, betraying the trust of you and your family. Your mother is coming to pick you up.

GO!

SHADOWS AND
TREASURES #3

You collapse on the chaise lounge in the corner of your Sanctuary and light a cigarette. Traveling across unraveling times, facing an alien Lucifer on his own turf, imprisoning a clawing creature in the Dungeon you strive to keep clean: these games take their toll. It's almost too much to handle.

You tip your decanter and Scotch splashes into your tumbler.

But you've done it.

Rest your bones, rest your body, rest your soul. You have earned it. But, first, unload yourself of your treasures. If you can call them that.

What I Found and I Hope You Did Too

I found at least five treasures in the last three games:

✓ **A talismanic chandelier**, definitely inhabited by some unworldly spirit. Unclear of its intentions, but seems like a good thing to keep around and to stay on the good side of.

✓ **A nugget of fool's gold.** You know what they say: a fool and his gold easily part, but fool's gold is a sure way to keep the fools at bay.

✓ **A sliver of Christ's cross.** Not something I ever expected to have in my possession but, if you had the chance to own this you probably wouldn't pass it up either.

✓ **An Indianapolis Stallions Big Game commemorative mug.**

✓ **The heart of a devil, plucked from the creature's chest while still beating in an attempt to save poor Drexxel:** Let's hope it worked!

✓ **Something Intangible.** There is something else, too, but I fear to tell you what it is. Some treasures lose their magic when you speak their names. Have you come across such an item as well?

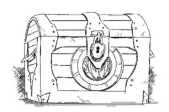

PREPARE YOURSELF

You have still have five games left. Do not face them lightly. Great things lie ahead.

THE ALAMO

"SANTA ANNA, I PRESUME," YOU SAY,

spitting on the dusty ground at the Mexican general's feet.

"Who the hell are you," he growls. "And how the hell did you get here?"

"I'm the guy who showed up to save the Alamo," you say. "And your time is up."

THE YEAR IS 1836. Tensions rise between Mexico and Texas, boiling over into a murderous battle from which very few will survive. But there's one thing no one counted on: that the Alamo's last hope would be a gun-wielding, badass time traveller with a desire to change history.

Welcome to the Past

Shifting pixelating prism-walls of the wormhole squiggle and snake past you as you walk forward through the disintegrating paradigms of your present-day life and into another time.

Into another world.

Not a brave new world.

No, not that. Instead, you walk into a brave old world.

The brave old world of Texas, to be exact. In the days before it was

officially part of the United States of America. The early days of the Year of our Lord 1836, in the time leading up to that tragedy known as The Battle of the Alamo.

You stand there, amongst the scuttlebugs and the croaking crickets, surveying the Alamo from the outside.

But you can only survey a fort for so long. It's time to approach. It's time to infiltrate.

You look in one direction. Then another. Then another. You keep looking for a while, trying to determine the next direction to look at because in the desert you can see in all directions, for miles.

Your Time Travel Logistics

Before you begin exploring the Alamo—before you introduce yourself to the guards, before you start shaking hands and donning a uniform, *before you get yourself a gun and kill yourself a bad guy*—it's important to consider what kind of a time traveller you are and what has motivated you to come back in time. Additionally, we have to spend some time considering what tremendous powers were able to send you back in time.

Here are a few of the most important questions for you to answer—or, if they prove too nebulous to answer, they must still be asked. For rhetoric's sake.

FROM WHAT YEAR HAVE YOU COME?

This is a simple one. I suggest that you choose a date later than 1996, as it should be a realistic time by which time travel has already been invented.

One difficult iteration of this is if you are a time traveller who has been scooped up by a different time traveller. We don't recommend playing this on your first attempt, as it adds another layer of challenge, but it is possible that you are a 1880s lumberjack who was kidnapped by an intrepid time traveller from the 2200s and then sent back to the 1830s to thwart time. A bit harder, yes, and so something we only recommend if you feel up to the challenge.

WHAT METHOD OF TIME TRAVEL BROUGHT YOU TO 1836?

Was is a timeship you climbed into? A wormhole invented by a scientist? An invention of your own making? Did you jump into a portal? Did you get frozen or phased in a chamber? Did your time travel require you to be nude, as is so often the case?

ARE YOU ABLE TO TRANSCEND BOTH TIME AND SPACE? OR ONLY TIME?

This might seem like a small detail, but worth considering. When you left your hometime for the Alamo in the Year 1836, were you able to do so from any place you wanted? Or did you have to go to the tourist trap, The Alamo, and, from there, you went back in time?

WHAT HAVE YOU BROUGHT WITH YOU?

Realistically, the answer to this will be *nothing*, as most time science relies on a "flesh and bone" system where only organic living matter can be transmitted. This means you will have to travel back to the Alamo in your most vulnerable state—*the nude.*

On a more positive note, this opens up the opportunity for an Animal Companion to accompany you. If you desire an Animal Companion for your mission, consult the Animal Companion Appendix at the end of this game.

Editors' Note: Unfortunately the "Animal Companion Appendix" was missing from this game as we found it, so it was difficult to figure out what animals the author originally intended for you to bring along on this mission. However, upon further playtesting we found that it's possible to bring along a multitude of animals of your choosing (including elephants) without drastically imbalancing the game.

HOW WILL YOU RETURN TO YOUR PRESENT DAY?

What is your escape plan? Is there one? Is your return to the present day dependent on your success here?

Do you have a device that will reverse your time travel? Or, if nude, do you know where to find one?

HOW MANY TIME TRAVELLERS HAVE THERE BEEN BEFORE YOU?

Are you the first? Or part of a crew?

Note that some of the missions you may be on can strongly correlate with this question, so you might not know the answer yet.

ARE THERE ANY COMPLICATED TIME PARADOXES OF WHICH YOU NEED TO BE AWARE?

Did you ensure you don't have any family members fighting on either side of the Alamo? If you do, are you prepared to act carefully and diplomatically to avoid a time paradox that tears your world apart?

AND, WHO SENT YOU?

Surely you have some idea forming here, but did you do this alone? Are you a time scientist? If so, it's important that you pause for a moment and work out a reasonable theory of time science that you are relatively confident could be achieved within your own lifetime, by you.

If this seems too daunting, consider instead how you might be a time traveller connected to a different time scientist who could have set this mission into motion. And is that time scientist connected to a board of other time travel directors somewhere? Are they good or evil? Are they governmental or rogue?

Your Disguise

You burst into the kitchen of the Alamo, facing the shocked looks of the staff. They wonder who you are and why you are nude.

"No time to explain!" you shout. "Give me an apron! And one of those fancy hats!"

While nudity may be acceptable in your hometime, in 1836 it is not. It's important to choose a disguise that will help you blend in with peoples of this era.

Be warned: obtaining a disguise should be one of your top priorities. If you do not find a disguise quickly, you may die from the elements, a wild animal attack, or you'll be shot dead on the spot.

TEXAN SOLDIER

An easy disguise, as there are many Texan soldiers in Texas. But you'll have to either kill (or seduce) a soldier without drawing blood to steal his clothes, blood being an indicator of wrongdoing. Or find an unused set of garb somewhere.

TOWNFOLK

Sure, it might be easy to find the clothes of a townsperson, or kill one in a bloodless manner, but will playing as a townsperson give you the requisite levels of access needed to accomplish your mission?

MEXICAN SOLDIER

Depending on your language skills and mission, finding a Mexican Soldier disguise could either be the perfect move or the path to reaching Game Over earlier than intended.

MEXICAN MERCENARY

Like the option above, but with more grit. As an advantage, this disguise will not be foiled if it's covered in blood.

CHEF

Playing this game disguised as a chef is a good way to fly under the radar, neutralizing your role from both sides of the battle. Although you may have to resort to using kitchen utensils as your weapons during the big fight.

Blood was a common sight on chef's clothes of this time period, which creates flexibility with how you obtain this disguise.

DAVY CROCKETT

Remember when you could watch Davy Crockett on television and imagine yourself living his adventures? Wearing his coonskin hat and carrying his musket? Well he's right here, at the Alamo.

If you can find Davy Crockett, bonk him over the head in a bloodless manner and steal his garb, then you'll solve both your immediate predicament and a lifelong ambition.

Your Mission

Now, there is one major question left, something we must explore at depth: **what is your mission as a time traveller sent to the Alamo?**

There are four primary motivations that might send a time traveller back, through the seas of time and to one of the greatest eras of bloodshed in the old West. Some of the answers you previously determined will help shape your mission, but the big question is yet to be answered.

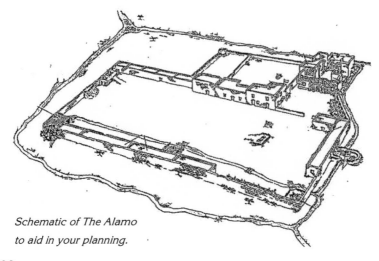

Schematic of The Alamo
to aid in your planning.

Now, your possible missions:

MISSION: SAVE THE ALAMO

The most straightforward of your possible missions.

To refresh yourself with the basic facts of the Alamo, it's good to remember that the Alamo is one of the most crushing defeats in Western history, rivaled only by the burning of the White House during the War of 1812, Custer's Last Stand at Little Big Horn, the sinking of the USS Maine in 1888, the bombing of Pearl Harbor by the Japanese in 1941, the entirety of the Vietnam and Korean wars, and all the other times that the United States have proven themselves to not be the pillar of strength and integrity that we would all like to believe.

If you choose to save the Alamo—or at least attempt to—here are a few of the reasons you may choose to do so:

❖ **The Patriotic Take:** You are a jingoistic, fired-up, red-blooded Texan who can't stand to think of your beloved homeland losing a battle—*any* battle. It keeps you up at the night, the idea that your boys were once lined up and shot by scoundrels from south of the border. So you're here. To change things.
❖ **The Savior Take:** There is a very simple reason you might want to save the Alamo: you think Davy Crockett is really cool and it makes you sad that he died. Knowing that he did not need to die could be motivation enough for you to go back and try to prevent his death. *Note: be sure not disguise yourself as him if your goal is to save him.*

MISSION: DEFEAT THE ALAMO

One other possibility, of course, is that you think the Alamo—while a crushing defeat during which every Alamo soldier present either died in battle or was executed by the end of it—was not a crushing *enough* defeat for the Texas Army.

The most difficult part of this argument is exactly how you can make the Alamo any more defeating. Everyone died. It's not like they can die more. But perhaps they can die quicker? Slower? Perhaps the Alamo could be burned down, or burned up, so there is nothing left to worship in the future?

Some reasons you might believe this:

❖ **Abolition:** one common argument, in later years, is that the Alamo was fought for the sake of protecting slavery. Mexico did not allow humans to enslave other humans and the United States, and the Republic of Texas, did. Having slaves is wrong.

101

- ❖ **Hubris:** Regardless of one's politics, it can be argued that the pre-battle Alamo represented humanity at its most delusional. Ideas like Manifest Destiny and aggressive expansion, burning and pillaging their way across the country like ants on a dying deer. Sure, is blood the answer to blood? Is death the response to death? Maybe, maybe not. It's up to you on how to view this.
- ❖ **Davy Crockett:** Some loved the man, but others, like you, perhaps, really hate him and want to kill him yourself. The fate of the Alamo be damned.

MISSION: RESEARCH THE ALAMO

There's always a need for more primary sources. Perhaps you come from an academic or intellectual institution, a board of professors or trustees who seek more information about one of the pivotal events in the history of Texas. You have gone back in time to gather data. Facts. The details.

This one could be boring, if you play it wrong. If you play it right, the possibilities are endless. Imagine the things you could see. The places you could go. The facts that you will discover that have not yet made it into the history books.

> **Editors' Note:** While researching the Alamo in the midst of battle was certainly exciting, with cannon balls flying around and whatnot, the time crunch created from the advancing Mexican Army put a heavy strain our academic pursuits. We recommend you set your time machine to 1835, to give you ample time to complete your research.

MISSION: UNDO PREVIOUS TIME TRAVELING

If there's one thing time travellers do, it's ruin things. Constantly. There's a good chance that you aren't the first time traveller to visit the Alamo and there's a good chance that whomever went before completely fucked things up. And there's an even better chance that that person was *you.*

Now you may not believe me, but **listen to my words**: this might not be the first time you've travelled back to the Alamo!

Imagine the repercussions of playing one of the other missions and then imagine what that could do to the timeline of America. Then, imagine how you would go back in time to prevent things from going awry.

Think about what you are willing to do. Will you kill someone in this other time? What if it's a fellow time traveller? How far are you willing to go?

What if your mission requires you to look yourself in the eyes and stab your time traveling self through the heart?

Time to Face The Alamo

JUST WHEN YOU THINK YOU'VE GOT EVERYTHING FIGURED OUT, AND YOUR MISSION IS CLEAR...

"You," someone says. "Pssst, you."

You look around, trying to find the source of the voice and then you see it. A head poking out from behind a cactus!

"It's not what you think!" the person says. "Just come here!"

And then the stranger steps out from behind the cactus and starts walking toward you. Your heart drops. Fear washes over you. You see that the man is wearing a duster, a cowboy hat, and completely nude underneath it all—a telltale sign that he too is a time traveller!

"That's right," the other time traveller says. "I'm what I look like. I know why you're here, because I'm here for the exact opposite reason."

Another time traveller? Now your mission is in jeopardy!

Six shooter loaded?

Disguise obtained, whether bloodlessly or not?

Mission objectives made clear?

Animal Companion by your side?

GO!!!

MURDER NIGHT

A WOMAN SCREAMS. A CHANDELIER FALLS.

A GUN FIRES IN THE DARKNESS.

And when the match is struck and the candle lit, a body lies before the surviving members of the dinner party. Someone suggests to check the pulse, but you already know it's too late.

Now comes the intrigue.

Who turned the living person into a dead body—and will the killer escape before the truth is discovered?

SEVEN STRANGERS GATHER AT A BARON'S ESTATE. Before the evening is up, one of them will be dead and one of them will have done it. With you, tangled in the midst of it.

London, 1906

Torrents of rain pummel your face as you run from the hansom cab to the manor's front gate. The estate looms large before you: a gothic and gargoyled monstrosity, its spires looming in the darkness. Lightning cracks and thunder rumbles through the land. An expanse of dark lawn stretches between the manor and the gate.

You stand at the gate, gusts of wind at your back, squinting through the wrought iron to see what lies on the other side.

Already the evening is awry—*how are you supposed to get to the other side of the fence? The gate is locked and every attempt to scale it results in you slipping back down onto the puddled ground. You are here for a dinner party, not a cat burglary.*

A dinner party, you remind yourself. Only a dinner party. Nothing to be nervous about, even if the exterior of this manor looks more menacing than you would have anticipated.

You look around for a bell when a hooded, hobbling man approaches the gate from the manor. He holds a lantern in his hands and, as he reaches you, you see his scarred gnarled face covered by a rat's nest of a beard. It chills you, not because of the scars but because you are certain you recognize this man but cannot say quite how.

"Come with me, good sir, for an elaborate feast awaits," the hooded strange man says.

You do as he commands, following this stranger toward the manor in the darkness, through the rain.

The Guests

Inside the manor the strange hooded man leads you, where your wet boots spill water across the opulent marbled floors. Through the long and winding halls you go to the Parlor Room.

And what a Parlor Room it is! Bustling with laughter and chit-chat, inside is the veritable who-is-who of rogues and socialites, characters whose reputations precede them (and not in a good way). You scan the room, taking in their faces, each of them posing as if their final portrait was being rendered right there and then.

STANDOR STEPHENSON

Rumored to be the illegitimate son of the duke seventeenth in line to the throne, Stephenson is known for his perpetual air of smug condescension and lavish living. Darker rumors swirl around him, including the suggestion that he blackmails the English nobility and uses the cash obtained to fund quixotic exploratory expeditions, with his greatest aim being landing a man on the moon in his lifetime. While one would expect his lunar ambitions to result in snickers at every turn, Stephenson is known to challenge *to the death* any man who laughs at him.

BUCKY BARLOW

The one American in the crowd, known for daring feats and a cavalcade of ex-lovers. Rumored to have been present at Kittyhawk when the Wright brothers discovered flight, only to quickly attempt to sell their methods to the Orient. Since the dawn of prohibition, he has spent more time in the British Isles with a focus on trading American-made automatic rifles for Irish whiskey and Scotch.

CALLIOPE CRANE

The operatic magician, notorious for the amount of male assistants who have drowned onstage during her most popular show's final illusion. Some have suggested that she is an archetypal "black widow", although there is no evidence that she was ever romantically involved with any of the men who've died under her watch. She has never been found guilty of any crimes and maintains high status for her social graces, beautiful singing voice, and full array of magical tricks.

Zephyr Xanadu

A mysterious and violent character, rumored by some to be from Egypt and by others the Arctic circle. The most widespread of the gossip around her has it that she travels the world as a professional dynamiter with a penchant for eliminating bridges, always available to whichever warring faction can pay the highest.

Chatsworth Chan

Half-Chinese. Half-Scottish. Full rogue. Evil tycoon, to boot. It's odd to see him in the same room as Stephenson, as one pervasive legend binds the men: Stephenson paid Chan for all the Chinese gunpowder it would take to reach the moon, and Chan promptly absconded to his father's homeland with the cash and Stephenson's ex-wife.

Helen Hayes

One of the first female barristers in the United Kingdom. You note, upon seeing her, that you've seen her name in the papers not just because she is famous for being the "lethal lady lawyer" but because she's defended, at one point or another, the rest of the characters in the room.

And then there is... *you*.

One might think it's odd to see *you* here, as your face has never graced the cover of a newspaper, let alone a wanted poster. You've never been called to trial, not as criminal or barrister or even witness. You are the anonymous face in this crowd.

But you knew this before you arrived. That's exactly why you're here.

The Host

Just as you have been observing the guests, they have been quietly watching you as well. They look you up and down for only a moment before Barlow resumes his tale of losing a ship of rum at the hands of pirates.

Not to be outdone, Calliope Crane sings in the other corner of the room, hitting high notes that force Bucky to tell his dashing tale with even more gusto.

You stand looking between the two small parties—Xanadu and Chan listening to Barlow while Stephenson admires the voice of Crane, with Hayes sitting peculiarly near the fire, not interacting—when the door behind you whooshes open again.

The hooded strange man stands in the threshold. Again, you are struck by how familiar he looks. You similarly wonder why you have been greeted by a hooded stranger rather than a butler or more conventional manservant.

And where, pray tell, is the host of the evening?

The stranger drops his hood and suddenly removes the false beard, already loose from the rain, and smeared makeup that had adorned his face previously: only to reveal Lord Kittridge Bloodington, the conniving lord and malevolent rail tycoon!

"I suppose you're wondering why I invited you here tonight under the utmost of secrecy," he says.

With those words, lightning cracks outside.

A Murder at Lord Kittridge Bloodington's Feast

"I have received a disturbing telegram earlier this week," Lord Bloodington says. "It provided me with the list of your seven names and said that at least one of us is marked for death on this very evening. Our lives are in deepest peril. I do not know whether it was threat or warning. But I knew I had to gather us here for a dinner party to clear this whole thing up and keep us safe."

The room erupts into questions, gasps, and hypothesizing. Fingers are pointed. Monocles slip from eyes.

Who would want one of us dead?

What has one of us done to deserve the assassin's hand?

But you know the answer, of course.

For it is you who is the assassin.

One of these rogues will die by your hand.

The Turn

Inside your jacket pocket is a sealed parchment you received earlier this week with your victims name printed upon it. So far, you have not broken that seal, but circumstances dictate that the time to reveal the name is now. Reach into your pocket, pull out the parchment, break the seal, and begin your plot.

GASP!

Where is the blasted parchment?! It was there moments ago, and it is certainly not in another pocket, either. Perhaps it was lost in your attempt to scale the fence, and has disintegrated in the torrential rain? Or did you leave it at home when you were getting dressed? Is it under the seat of the hansom cab?

With your parchment gone and no hope of retrieval, your mission seems to come to an abrupt end. You may wish to simply enjoy the evening and leave killing to another day.

However, if you wish to continue with your mission, whether under threat of death or some other assassin's code, there is a still a chance you may deduce who your target is, much like a detective would, by reexamining the circumstances which led you here in the first place.

An Assassin Trained for Just This Task

No one becomes an assassin without some hard work and an assortment of chance encounters that shaped them into who they are today.

There are a few questions you have to ask. Specifically:

I.   What length of time have you been assassinating for?
II.   Who are you associated with?
III. What first drew you to the murder business?

Now, let's dive in and flesh this out.

WHAT LENGTH OF TIME HAVE YOU BEEN ASSASSINATING FOR?

SHORT
You're a rookie, having killed only once, accidentally, or perhaps even never. And so tonight is a very big night: you have to prove yourself, both to yourself and to the people who are counting on you to make this murder happen.

This means the missing parchment is a very big deal. If you don't figure out who to kill and make sure they die, you might have to find an entirely new career. Even worse, you could end up dead yourself.

MEDIUM
A body here, a body there, but you still pick up non-murder odd jobs to keep the lights on. You've got a few murders under your belt but not enough for a pension. It's definitely unlike you to lose a target's name, and your career trajectory will flatline if word gets out.

LONG

You are fully committed to making Murder your legacy, which means you're going to stick this one out to the end and make sure the right person and *only* the right person dies tonight. Grab a cup of espresso and get down to details.

EXTRAORDINARILY LONG

The puppy stopped breathing. You didn't know you had killed it just yet, because of course a three year old has no concept of *Murder*. But after growing up, getting an education in school, and killing a few more along the way, Murder is now crystal clear to you and you've been doing it ever since.

Deducing the name on the parchment is of little concern to you, because you can always just kill them all.

QUITE SOME TIME, BUT NOW ON HIATUS, AND ONLY BACK FOR ONE LAST MURDER

You knew this was a bad idea. You had the cottage in Dover, a grandchild bouncing on your knee, a pipe you smoke every evening as you gaze at the stars. And you threw it all away to be here, now, amongst these scoundrels.

Of course you lost the parchment. Your heart was never in this. Perhaps you can sneak away with your life and your dignity still intact.

WHO ARE YOU ASSOCIATED WITH?

A GANG OF STREET THUGS

Hailing from the harbours on the Thames, you and your street crew never say no to a contract that pays. You usually like to handle assassinations rough, but you'll make a special exception tonight and leave your knuckle dusters at the door.

SECRET SERVICE BUREAU

Law and order must rule eternally, and by your hand you will do anything to uphold it—even if that means committing illegal homicide. You specialize in taking out Guerilla Fighters that seek to harm your colonies abroad.

Personal Revenge Killing

You work alone, known for your discretion and your abilities to eliminate the wicked souls who've earned death. Your clients are too angry for blackmail and wealthy enough to afford you. You like to think of yourself as a High Society Murderer, killing with poison and charm. A job will come your way and you'll get it done, with a smile and a wink.

Pilot's Union

Air travel is the most coveted technology of this time, and as such, Pilots have banded together to eliminate all who wish to see their buzzing contraptions swatted from the skies. You've lost count of how many people you've pushed from zeppelins, how many parachutes you've tampered with, in the name of air travel.

Usually, you fight from above: so tonight, on the ground, you're out of your element.

Wizard's Guild

This roving band of mystics and psychics performs many miracles and feats using their powers of hypnosis, but many would prefer if they just vanished in their own disappearing act.

Sworn enemies of the Catholic Church and other institutions of power, like the government. Known for wicked sacrifices in subterranean lairs and great taste in pocket watches. If you are a member of the Wizard's Guild, you use powerful tricks of hypnosis and sleight of hand, like juggling.

A Stranger in an Alley

This is how all your jobs find you. You're minding your own business, when someone appears in front of you, out of the darkness, and growls: *it's time for another one.* The parchment is always delivered in this manner. You collect the name, do the deed, and collect your cash.

WHAT FIRST DREW YOU TO THE MURDER BUSINESS?

Choose at least one of the following:

- Money
- Fame
- Desperation
- Psychotic Episode

- Someone Knew a Terrible Truth About You And Extorted You Into Committing Your First Murder
- Kill for Me or I'll Kill You
- Kill for Me and I'll Kill for You
- You Were in Debt to a Villain and Could Only Pay Him in Murder
- A Sale on Knives
- A Sale on Dynamite
- Faulty Dynamite
- You Were a Dynamite Salesman and Didn't Know What to Do With the Extra Dynamite
- You're a Gun Salesman and it's Not Your Fault what People Do with Your Products
- A Dare
- An Accident You Took Credit For and Now Everyone Thinks You're In The Murder Business
- You're Not in the Murder Business; You're Just Covering for a Friend
- Military Training Provided Real World Job Opportunities
- Just Trying to Earn Some Extra Cash So You Could Fix Up Your Dungeon
- You're A Dungeon Lord and Wanted to Make Some Money Out of Your Empty Dungeon.
- It's the Family Business
- It's Not Your Family Business Originally But You Married Into It
- Peer Pressure: Your Friends Were All Assassins and You Wanted to Fit In
- Expensive Tastes That Can Only Be Afforded With Blood Money
- You're Not One to Pass Up a Major Career Opportunity, Even if it Includes Murders

---

Last Ditch Effort: How many pockets do you have?

Check every pocket to ensure the parchment is indeed lost. This is a futile gesture but something you can do to feel better. Try turning your pockets inside out, thoroughly emptying them of every last ball of dust. Then, check them all over again, one more.

Check your footwear and your hat while you're at it. Is it possible you hid it in your pocket watch? Behind your ear? Bottom of the shoe?

Time to Read The Room

Lighting strikes once again, for the umpteenth time this evening. Dinner—the centerpiece of which is the head of a boar, pear in mouth—is served. The eight of you sit at the dining room table, with the host at one end and you at the other.

You wonder how odd the other guests must find it that you, the one unknown guest, are at one end of the table. Are they suspicious of you yet?

Using the clues you've learned from the circumstances which have drawn you here tonight, you listen as the conversation progresses around you and attempt to see if anything lines up, or if anyone is more nervous than normal after receiving the news that their life is in peril.

You weigh the truths of their existences...

- Is **Standor Stephenson** deserving of death? How many men has he killed in a duel? How many more must die in his mission to reach uncharted lands? Has he crossed your employer in such a way that you were dispatched to dispose of him?
- **Bucky Barlow** might seem dashing and mysterious, but can any good come of his arms trading and booze running? If you were the one at the bullet's end of his gun, would he hesitate for a moment? How many may want him dead?
- What is the truth of all these men who died under **Calliope Crane's** magical mistakes? Is she just unlucky? Are they? What is the truth of her existence, and could the family of one of her dead assistants have hired an assassin to dispatch her?
- How many bridges has **Zephyr Xanadu** destroyed? How many wars were changed forever because of her skills with dynamite and no-questions-asked approach to her jobs? Could a defeated general be behind your hiring, intending to finish her off? Or perhaps someone who wants to keep her quiet?
- Did the ever-conniving confidence man **Chan** finally meet his consequences? Do you wear the mask of his death?
- Who doesn't want **Helen Hayes** dead, either for something she did or something she knows?

As always, a careful choice is required. More than ever before, the wrong move has the deadliest of consequences.

Is It Time to Come Clean?

The guests consume the feast with ferocity as they know it might be their last.

But you? Not a bite.

The overwhelming guilt bubbles up inside and the confusing swirl of clues crash down and scatter in the wind. Nothing makes sense in your head!

You admit it to yourself: you're a killer. Not a dinner guest. You have failed! And the only way out is confession.

COMING CLEAN

First of all, you don't have to come clean. This is an optional final section.

Are you tired of this charade? Would you like to clear your conscience? You can admit to everyone that you are an assassin and that you would like to escape from this terrible situation. Perhaps they will forgive you. Perhaps this is the end of your career. And perhaps it is time.

You should only play this option if you cannot determine your victim based on the above clues *and* if you have not been assassinating for *Extraordinarily Long*.

WHERE AND WHEN TO COME CLEAN

If you choose to come clean, it can occur either during **dinner, dessert, or digestifs.**

If this is your approach, please ensure it occurs before the guests are putting their coats on or have had too much to drink.

```
┌─────────────────────────────────────────────────────────┐
│        Last Ditch Effort: Come Clean (Variant)          │
│     This is the same option as above, but it is a bluff. │
│                                                          │
│  In this option, you are coming clean not to genuinely   │
│  cleanse yourself but, instead, to create one final      │
│  opportunity to gauge their reactions and see if the     │
│  confession stirs any one guest more than the others.    │
│                                                          │
│      This is a second chance to Read The Room!          │
└─────────────────────────────────────────────────────────┘
```

Murder weapon in pocket?

Still missing the scrap of parchment?

Knowledge of your alliances and the length of time you've been assassinating for?

Ready to kill? And if not, *to come clean?*

GO!

YOUR JOB

THE CONVEYOR BELT COMES TO LIFE.

You can smell soldering irons and sawdust, hear the chirps and squeaks and klaxons that fill the grind of your daily work life.

Down the belt come the typical items: chrome widgets and titanium micro-units, chestplate iron-sprockets and zig-zag cables. You begin to zone out, falling into a routine, hearing the chatter between men and machine somewhere distant behind you.

Then—something comes down the conveyor belt that attracts your attention. A new item, not something you've ever seen before or would ever expect to see. Not here. Not anywhere.

You pick up the item and stare at it. An item made in the factory where you work.

*You stare at an artificial replication of **your own face.***

> Smalltown, Minnesota. 2042. YOUR GOAL: DO YOUR JOB. You punch the clock daily in a factory that produces all the items used to increase autonomy and eliminate the need for such factories. Every day, slowly but surely, you make your own job less necessary. Today, you begin to question what lies at the end of this dark path.

119

Your Hometown, as it exists today

Another Day At Work

BRRRZZZT. The klaxon sounds and all the factory workers step away from their positions. After a long day at work, Pete Bogfellow, the foreman, wipes his brow and gives you a piece of his mind: "Say, this factory, these fine products, it's all I've ever known. I don't know if I could give them up."

"Excuse me?" you might say, needing more context. The two of you walk to a social gathering point.

"You didn't hear? Tomorrow they're announcing the layoffs. Say they've got some new automatons that might be replacing a few of us. Now, I've put my blood, sweat and tears into this company. Not one sick day. Not one vacation taken. I got 124 days saved up, and I didn't do all this for nothing! I chose to go here. I chose to stay in this town with my wife, start a family, have children that depended on me to support them. I could've gone off to corporate, worked that plush office job down in North Carolina. But I didn't. Guess you could say I gave it all up for them."

A few other factory workers approach, removing their work gear, all eager to share their thoughts on the upcoming changes to the company.

One of your fellow workers looks you to and asks: "Hey, what do you think about all this?"

CREATING A CHARACTER

In order to answer your co-worker's question effectively, it's important you know your role in this company and your opinions about what's happening all around you.

WHAT THEY PAY YOU TO DO

You work in a factory, as we've established. What we have to establish now is what you do at the factory. This job is crucial for the economic well-being of you and your family, and the experience granted by it may help you in your battle against obsolescence.

Choose from one of the seven professions:

MOVER

*"I needed those ten boxes of **Zoop Zoops** at the other side of the factory five minutes ago!", cries the Foreman. With a sense of pride, you strap on your waistband and your leather gloves: it's time for work!*

The mover is a heavy-lifting and simple minded workhorse upon which the rest of the factory stands. When someone needs something moved, or something is blocking your path, it's up to you to move it. They're strong armed and strong willed. Great for beginners.

Starting Equipment: Leather Gloves, Waistband, Packing Tape, Barcode Scanner.

WELDER

*Light flickers off your visor and sparks ricochet. A thought crosses your mind: Everything on this Earth is connected together in some way, but no one knows just how. But when it comes to these **Jiggerydoos** and **Plunketts**, there's a very specific point that's clearly indicated where you'll need to fuse them together. What if everything had clearly indicated markings? Could you connect the whole world?*

Dexterous and skilled. Quick movements, precise actions, and a life of developing the skills required of the labor. A pyrotechnician on a micro scale, Welders can combine any two materials and make them one. Great for characters focused on the assembly floor.

Starting Equipment: Welding Mask, Blowtorch, Leather Apron, Cigar.

SCIENTIST

*If only the **Dinkleheimers** that connected the legs joints to the hips of your robotic brethren weighed 5% less, they'd save hours of battery power. What if you could create a material that weighed less? Test tubes in hand, you carefully pour and mix volatile solutions together... one false move and this whole factory goes up in flames!*

You possess information, knowledge, and critical thinking skills that those around you do not have. You understand that these machines are programmed to act and think like men, but lack the capacity of emotion, making them no more than metal golems. This strong intellect makes you a quick thinker. However, your weak musculature makes you susceptible to strong blows.

Starting Equipment: Prescription Glasses, Lab Coat, Pocket Protector, Calculator, Sustenance Capsules, ID Card, and a Pocket Full of Random Tools.

RECEPTIONIST

No artificial face can take your job—because you, of course, are the face of the company!

KaboOm! An explosion erupts from deep within the factory, and you still have four guests waiting in the lobby, each filing their own grievances over their severance pay! As you wipe the excess water from the fire sprinklers away from your computer screen, you rapidly rearrange their meeting schedules. But one task remains: evacuating them to safety.

Everything has its place and it's your job to find it. You are a great mediator, an incredible lover, and always striving to create order in the center of chaos that we call life. Your loyalty to the company comes above all else: in a world dominated by robots, studies have shown that customers always prefer human face-to-face contact when entering a business encounter.

Starting Equipment: Holo-Terminal, Breath Mints, Post-it Notes, Coffee-Room Key, Intruder Alert Kill-Switch Radio.

MIDDLE MANAGEMENT

*Human error is inevitable, and it's your job to find the root cause. You've got four workers handling the die-cast **Klunkerbuns** and six workers loading code onto the programmable **Yorpols** and two hundred workers scrambling to quality control the thousands of **Fzlifszn-Kryzgiznsz** that are barreling towards the assembly line. Now, they could easily create a faulty run of **Chungles**, but would robotic hands do much better? If so, would you still have a job?*

Look, this isn't a real job, but on paper it looks like one. No one listens to you when you tell them "Great job!" and your "four point success strategy" doesn't seem to be catching on. You can tell everyone is happiest when you sit in your office alone and play games, so you're working on a "three-point strategy" that keeps things that way. You work best when there's no work to do.

Starting Equipment: Photo of your Family.

123

MACHINE WHISPERER

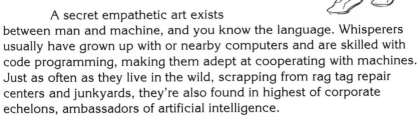

You can tell when a machine is in pain: A lowly **Bogfloob** bot hasn't worked in days, and no one knows why. With a quiet voice, you whisper, "Bleep bloop" into its top intake manifold. The **Bogfloob** shudders, almost in response. You run your fingers along the beveled edges of its control panel, and you hear a whimper coming deep from inside. "Lil' fella."

You try again, mustering all your energy. It's not right for them to feel like this. "BLEEP BLOOP!" you yell into its tuba-shaped orifice. With a cough and a gag, the machine rumbles to life!

A secret empathetic art exists between man and machine, and you know the language. Whisperers usually have grown up with or nearby computers and are skilled with code programming, making them adept at cooperating with machines. Just as often as they live in the wild, scrapping from rag tag repair centers and junkyards, they're also found in highest of corporate echelons, ambassadors of artificial intelligence.

Starting Equipment: A deep sense of empathy and a backstory involving a machine saving the life or dignity of you or a family member.

ENDO-MAN

Heads turn as you enter the assembly floor, and everyone's body language tells you that something is afoul. 51 organic eyes lock onto you in rapid succession, and the look they're giving you is unmistakable: you are not alike. You hear a whispering, voices, so you increase the sensitivity on your sensors, and the voices become clear.

"What happened to him?" or "He looks like a fax machine!" or "There's no way he's a real man."

You sit down at your stool in front of the conveyor belt, when **Gglorps** and **Theebles** begin rushing up to your station... too many to assemble for a normal man. But you are an ENDO-MAN! Your mechanical hands splinter into articulated dozens, sorting them faster than anyone around you. This is <u>YOUR JOB!</u>   (con't)

Endo-Men are cyborgs designed for the factory lifestyle. They're created when normal men suffer tragic life-changing injuries and are forced to meld with machine to survive. This creates certain advantages for them. They are modified to have one of the following abilities: Increased Running Speed, Increased Upper Body Strength, Increased Dexterity, Increased Intelligence.

Starting Equipment: Factory Smock.

What Your Factory Makes

Gglorps? Theebles? What are all these crazy things and why would anyone ever make them?

They're not crazy things. Clearly it's your first day on the job.

These are the items your factory makes. It's important that you understand how everything works before you begin.

> EMPLOYEES ARE REQUIRED TO MEMORIZE EACH OF THESE ITEMS AND THEIR USES.

1. **Zoop Zoops:** Tension-infused metal coils for data pad management
2. **Jiggerydoo:** Lithium rod outfitted with a balance receptor
3. **Plunkett:** Multipurpose housing with internal voltage control
4. **Dinkleheimer:** Spherical gelatin with metallic flake for low amperage signal transmission
5. **Klunkerbuns:** Smooth data-infused plating
6. **Yorpol:** Versatile micro computers
7. **Fzlifszn-Kryzgiznsz:** Hinged flex antennae that come in A, B, and C configurations
8. **Chungles:** Intelligent belligerent automatic repair units
9. **Bogfloob:** A coal powered multi function assembly traffic operator
10. **Gglorps:** Male couplers for plasma transmission
11. **Theebles:** Double female receptors for plasma transmission
12. **Aeliofrills:** Quad independent arms that double as propellers
13. **Menkoon:** Foam strandings that facilitate moisture transfer
14. **Smunk:** A cubic non-newtonian fluid fuels calculating cortexes
15. **Deltrox 429:** A gravity-defying powder designed for human use
16. **V.D.O.2.P.Q.L.Kenny:** Small AI companion that helps guide human workers through assembly floor

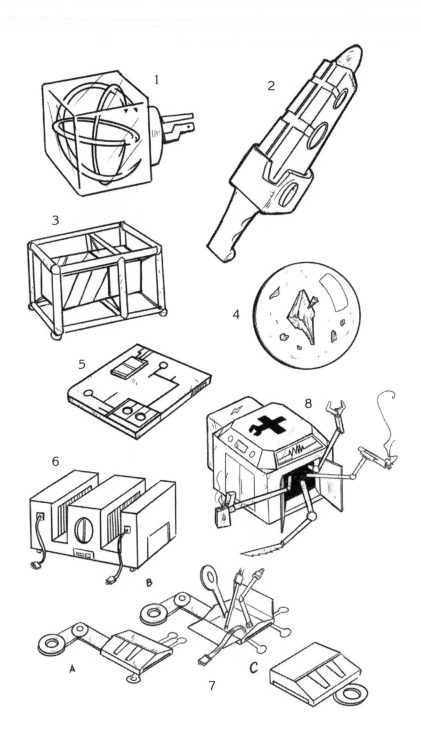

1

2

3

4

5

6

7

8

A

B

C

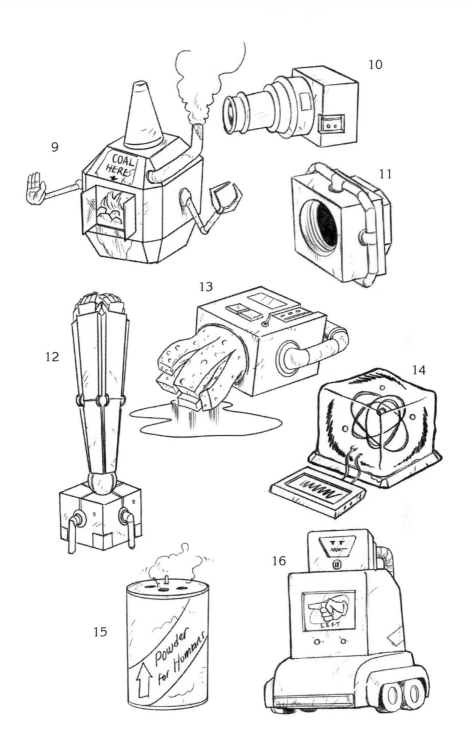

9

10

11

12

13

14

15

16

Your Alignment on The Machines and Your Opinion of Them

Machines have not ascended all the way to man's station, of course, and this is something you will argue about at the bar with the boys or around the water cooler or around the Thanksgiving dinner table where you gather with diverse family members and debate the truths of this world.

There are three popular opinions regarding the current situation of the world and, in particular, your town.

As described earlier, this game begins with a debate about this subject breaking out in a social setting, the night before a significant change is about to take place at your work. Please choose one of these opinions:

> **Anti-Machine:** They run the entirety of society. We are their slaves now.
> **Machine-Neutral:** The machines are not as serious of a risk as we might think. They're nothing more than overgrown toasters.
> **Pro-Machine:** They are neither overlords nor afterthoughts. Machine rights is a major concern and being a Machine Rights Activist is the only true path forward.

While it's up to you to expand these opinions into full debates—and to both imagine and anticipate what direction your friends, coworkers, and acquaintances may take these in—you should consider some of the most common arguments and where you fall.

This is your Alignment—how others will judge your actions, where you fall during debates and, potentially, in the events to come.

OPINION #1: MACHINES ARE IRRELEVANT; OR, MACHINE-NEUTRAL

Many members of the town argue that the machines are not as big of a deal as one might think. As of now, this is still the most prevalent, although each the other two are gaining ground in this town.

Machines comes in various forms throughout the town, although one known fact is that they cannot and do not come in the form of human look-alikes... *yet.*

128

They tend to be slow, trudging buckets of bolts and aluminum, doing menial tasks like putting carts away at the supermarket or even conducting the act of grocery shopping for the wealthy and elderly and lethargic, who prefer to stay home and allow machines to do their bidding.

A few common talking points used by people with the Machine-Neutral alignment:

- "Are you afraid of your toaster? Your washing machine? These are not different."
- "A few minor precautions are all it takes to ensure that machines won't ever cause trouble, like installing 'off' buttons."
- "Wake me up if real robots are invented. Until then, don't worry."
- "Honestly, it wouldn't hurt to have an extra hand once in a while on the assembly floor. I think we could make a great team, machines and I."

As stated before, this is the most popular viewpoint, but that doesn't necessarily make it correct. That said, it does tend to be the viewpoint people are most comfortable espousing.

OPINION #2: MACHINES ARE THE EVIL OVERLORDS;
OR, ANTI-MACHINE

An increasingly common belief in this town. Those who believe this tend to whisper about it while avoiding any kinds of technology, as to avoid technology is the only way to ensure that a machine is not reading one's communications or mind.

This means no hyper-beepers, no compu-feeds, no e-letters—not even telephone calls.

If you are of this ilk, you are likely to refer to them as "robots", a label that those in Option #1 tend to consider silly and those in Option #3 consider offensive.

Some talking points for the Anti-Machine:

- "We cannot trust them. Look at how much has changed in our lifetimes. So much more will change, and if we trust them now then they will kill us tomorrow."
- "They are studying our every move. Even if they seem harmless, they're not."

- "Didn't you hear about the farmer who had the accident with his automatic thresher in Iowa? Does that count as a robot? I think it counts. That thresher *wanted* to kill him."
- "Think twice before kicking that toaster, because it may remember that, and one day grow legs to kick you back. *And that's why I hate them!*"
- "This is *my* paycheck and is *my* job. Stay away from my life!"

In certain circles there is a tendency to pretend that one is Machine-Neutral, even when one is Anti-Machine, because of a pervasive belief that the machines will begin rounding up and imprisoning all humans.

There is another, more extreme, version of this belief, which is that they've already completed this task and everyone is living their life oblivious to this.

OPINION #3: MACHINES NEED OUR HELP;
OR, PRO-MACHINE

In stark contrast to the Anti-Machine belief, there are many Machine's Rights Activists who believe that that machines are innocent creatures who need our help to survive and may even assist us in transcending our own humanity.

To better understand this, consider that machines are increasingly sentient. As you read this—you, somewhere in the 1990s, in your crazy world of honks and beeps—it might be hard to transport yourself into a future where every fax machine has legs and can talk.

But in Smalltown, Minnesota, in the year 2042, you better believe fax machines can talk! While the first party would think this is a silly novelty and the second consider them to be elements of evil, the Machine Rights Activists are in the camp that a talking fax machine is a creature deserving of sympathy, care, protection, and even a postmodern form of Platonic love.

Here are some talking points for those who lean Pro-Machine:

- "These are sentient beings that we created and, thus, we are responsible for. Would you abandon your own children?"
- "Imagine if God disowned Man when Man became too powerful. Should Man do the same to Machine?"
- "It's time to award the Machines with voting rights and citizenship so that they take themselves seriously as our allies and potential family members."

- "Think twice before kicking that toaster, because it may remember that, and one day grow legs to kick you back. *And it would have every right to.*"
- "I always hated my job in this factory and would rather have a machine take my job, giving me more time to create art and music and explore the higher purposes of my humanity."

The Pro-Machine crowd includes certain subsets, including the more militant Machine Rights Activists and the pacifist Alliance for Allies of Non-Humans.

Consider, now, how nuanced any one opinion can be.

LET'S RECAP

Before proceeding, make sure you've answered the following questions:

1. What is YOUR JOB at the factory?
2. What is your opinion of the machines?
3. Is Pete Bogfellow your friend or foe?
4. Do your values conflict with your work environment?

BACK AT WORK

All your co-workers continue to stand silently, awaiting your reply.

After taking moment to collect your thoughts, you finally feel prepared to respond to your co-worker's question about what you think about all this. And as such, you explain your nuanced opinion on it all.

Think through exactly how you would articulate your opinion. Imagine the looks on the faces of your coworkers as they listen. Do they nod their heads or shake them? Is a chorus of yeas or nays? How does it go over?

"Huh," says ol' Pete Bogfellow, "Never thought of it that way."

You return home and get a good night's rest, feeling contented and as if you have reached a satisfying resolution. At the very least, it appears your social dynamics at work are solid and friendly, even if you and your coworkers represent a large range of skill sets and political opinions.

THE BIG DAY: THE ARRIVAL OF THE ENDO-MEN

The next day begins and you head to work. Armed with the confidence of job security, you pull down the lever that punches your time card. You begin the work day with your locker room routine of donning your uniform, but can instantly tell something is amiss: workers gather around good ol' Pete Bogfellow, once again.

He's reading aloud a letter he received.

"It is with our deep regret that we must begin the termination of all non-essential employees, to make way for the next development of our corporation. We will always appreciate the hard work and dedication shown by our team members, but unfortunately it still was not enough to compete with the efficiency and discipline of their automaton counterparts: The Endo-Men."

*Pete slowly looks up to **you**, as do the rest of the workers.*

*"Was it **you** who did this? Sell us out for those...abominations? These were our jobs. Now what are we supposed to do!?"*

*Whether it was or wasn't you, you have no time to answer, because all the locker room doors open at once, and in flood lines of **Endo-Men**, encircling and trapping the group!*

*"**You are not essential!!**" says one Endo-Man as he violently grabs Pete by the collar and drags him out of the room, screaming!*

The room erupts into chaos as all non-essential employees are forced out of the factory.

You gulp as an Endo-Man picks you out of the crowd, about to deliver the news of your future...

Everything you've ever known has just come to a halt... or has it? You still have your skills and your opinions. What happens next in your story?

The choice is yours. Carefully decide your next move, and how you will react to the news, whether good or bad. Major things—perhaps your life or, even worse, perhaps your job—are at stake.

GO!

SHADOWS AND
TREASURES #4

How strange you find it that—even if you had chosen to play as an Endo-Man—you still find something inherently wrong with a robot replacing Your Job, and your programming allows you to be an Anti-Machine Machine.

And so, now you stand in your Sanctuary, beholding your small box of treasures.

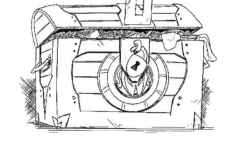

Each treasure tells a tale. Each one holds a memory, some false and some true. Those treasures, those memories, are what made you who you are today.

Do you recall you who were at the beginning of this journey?

Do not relax yet. The battles are not won.

Gently, gingerly, cautiously, place your treasures in the box and make sure that they are not broken.

Close the treasure box.

Go to the door of the Sanctuary.

Leave. We will return here once more.

CHESS

On the battlefield of black and white,

the reign of the King comes to its end. He and his few remaining soldiers stand with their backs against the wall, their ranks diminished, their morale deflated.

The spears and swords of the fierce enemy soldiers draw near. A final thought comes to the King's mind as he watches death close in.

"In my dreams, I dreamed of two kings leading two armies together," he muses. "I knew our unification would come at a great cost, but I never expected that my death would be the price to pay."

A gleam of light dances across the King's dagger as it begins to slip from his weak hand. The King looks down and studies the blade, its sharp edge dulled after years of rule. This dagger was once a great sword, a magnificent blade that struck down all those who stood between him and the crown. But each life he took whittled the sword down to the meager shard that now lies in his palm.

He looks up to see an enemy bishop staring at him from a crooked angle. And not far from the bishop, an enemy knight looks ready to pounce. This is it. The King must answer for his crimes.

"Hark, Emperor!" a voice cries, four paces to his right. The King looks up with joy! He is not alone!

In a whoosh of a black cape, an ally dives in front of the King! It's Chatwick, a castle (rook) of a man and one of strongest of his army. He's bloody and beaten but still alive. The King's dull eyes light up. The Black Flame rises once again. This fight is far from over!

Chess is an ancient two-player game of strategy, played using a checkerboard except the playing pieces are based on roles commonly found in a medieval monarch's court.

A Quiet Game on a Rainy Summer's Eve

You are expecting a visitor this evening. A guest, a companion. A friend, perhaps. Perhaps something more than a friend or perhaps the antithesis of a friend. Perhaps an enemy, a villain, a shadow.

There are many people—both friends and strangers—that could visit you this evening. It really just depends who you've invited. Or, who is bold enough to stop by unannounced.

The rain falls in sheets. It's no surprise why you've decided to stay in and play a board game instead of go out.

One specific game: **Chess**.

SETTING THE SCENE

- ❖ **Where am I?** What city are you in? What room? We know that it is a summer evening and that rain falls from the sky, but do you watch the rain fall from a living room window? A cramped apartment? A three-season porch? Under a bridge wrapped in newspapers? At a café in Paris?
- ❖ **When am I?** You are welcome to play this game in any era, as long as you don't choose an era so ancient that Chess has not been invented yet.
- ❖ **How am I?** Generally speaking, how is your health? Have you had enough sleep, in case the game goes long into the night?
- ❖ **Who am I?** The eternal question, is it not? It could be you. Chess can also be played as a subgame in any other of the games we've presented, so you may be a cowboy or a small child.

The Opponents

Someone knocks on the door of wherever you are. You stand to answer. It is your opponent.

136

Tonight you will be playing Chess against one of the following:

- ➢ The Child (Easy)
- ➢ The Lost Love (Intermediate)
- ➢ The Machine (Hard)
- ➢ The Shadow (Expert)

Before you choose which of these four you would like to play against—before you can answer the door—the memory of your first childhood game of Chess washes over you, determining the confidence and strategy with which you play the game of Chess.

Your Mentor

Or, Establishing Your Chess Story

"Just move the pieces, like this," says your mentor.

You move the pieces as he says. He quickly takes them out with his Knight.

"You still have much to learn," he says.

There are things you can control and things you can't control in this game.

One thing that you cannot control is your age when Chess first enters your life: you are a child, a young precocious child who has repeatedly learned that the athletic field is not for you. You might enjoy watching baseball games, or at least the idea of watching baseball games, but that does not mean that you can play the game itself, not when you step up to the plate in physical education class and miss the ball once again.

But then there was something that you could excel at. Something you could win at, dominate, use to your advantage to shape your present and your future. (Or at the very least, understand and know the basic rules.) The beautiful, antique, strange and magical game of Chess.

NOW YOU HAVE A MENTOR

"Say, kid, you fancy a game?" a strange man says to you.

"I don't know, I'm running late for piano class." you reply.

"That's ok. I'll teach you the rules real quick."

You didn't just learn Chess from a rule book. You learned it from a Chess master.

Chess masters come in all shapes and sizes, but ultimately there are only three archetypes that they eventually fall into.

Who was *your* Chess master?

- ❖ **The Cool Guy in the Park:** A cool, hip guy who talked fast and played speed Chess in the park. He bet cash and schooled rubes, and was always surrounded by chattering crowds watching him in awe.
- ❖ **A Stuffy Academic:** A wise old master who prized decorum and etiquette. He believed in the fundamentals, in the studying of past games, and wanted you to do the same.
- ❖ **A Mysterious Russian:** A frightening, gaunt foreigner who taught Chess with cruelty and spite—but ultimately turned out to have a heart of gold.

Any of these three mentors are equally valid, in terms of learning the rules of Chess. But, it's important to note that whomever did teach you Chess will ultimately return to haunt the entirety of your life as a lingering ghost, standing over your shoulder and giving you advice during every game you play.

Now that it's established who first taught you Chess we must discuss the rules themselves.

The Chess Board

"You'll never succeed with that attitude," says your mentor, a saying all mentors say, regardless of their archetype. "And you have to know the fundamentals before you can try the tough stuff."

So, let's get into the fundamentals.

This is what a Chess board looks like, and where the Chess pieces go.

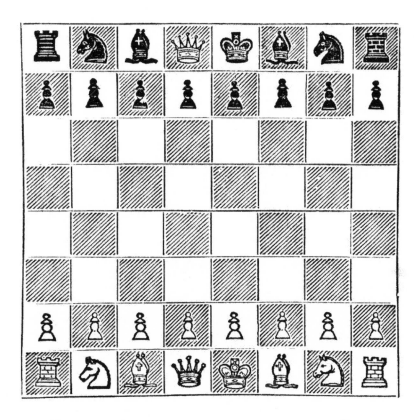

You may struggle with a desire to set up the board differently than its intended usage. It's common to wonder what it would be like to play with different pieces, a larger board, or to mix up starting positions of the knights and the bishops.

The Chess Pieces

"You move the pieces," your mentor says, "but that doesn't mean they can move anywhere you want. Stop trying to make the knight fly from one side of the board to the other. He'll never move that way. Now, your move."

You move a piece.

"Then I move. Then you move again."

There are things you have to learn: don't try to take two turns in a row; don't try to move your opponent's piece; don't castle a second time; don't keep an extra Queen literally hidden up your sleeve.

And so it works as such: you and your opponent take turns moving a single piece of your designated color. Each style of piece has its own special rules and abilities—including its own way of attacking. When you attack an opponent's piece, and succeed, your opponent loses that piece.

"They each follow the official rules of their piece," your mentor says. "Memorize them."

Here are the pieces and what they do:

King, Queen, Bishop, Knight, Castle (rook), Pawn

- **KING** - The eldest of the pieces, moving 1 space at a time *(with the exception of The Castle, a move we will discuss later)*
- **QUEEN** - The quickest and deadliest of pieces, moving straight in any direction. All other pieces wish they were the Queen, although they live to serve the King.
- **BISHOP** - God moves in mysterious ways, and in this case, at an angle. This piece moves any number of spaces diagonally.
- **KNIGHT** - The cavalry, moving 3 paces then turning 1 to either side, oft giving the impression of flying over the other pieces. *(Careful not to fly too far.)*
- **CASTLE (rook)** - Moves any number of spaces, straight or sideways. *(The Castle walls sometimes defend the King, allowing him to trade spaces and take refuge inside them.)*
- **PAWN** - Marches 1 pace forward per turn. May sneak in an extra space on its first turn, and may only attack at a frontward-diagonal angle.

Advanced players may also wish to consider including these pieces into their game:

Shied, Archer, Jester, Prince Harold

- **SHIELD** - A wide piece taking up two spaces that can only move side to side one space per turn. Invulnerable and cannot attack.
- **ARCHER** - May only move forward one space at a time, and may strike opponents that are 2 spaces away in any direction.
- **JESTER** - Taunts opponents by encircling them, moving freely about the board regardless of turn.
- **PRINCE HAROLD** - A spry boy of only 13 with golden hair who is heir to the throne. His goal is to find his mother, the Queen, and convince her to stop this war at once. He has never seen battle before, so is able to move any number of spaces, as long as he's not headed towards combat.
- **DUNGEON** - A piece that is 3x3 tiles large and permanently imprisons the piece it surrounds. It begins the game out of play and is placed into the game at the player's discretion at any time. It cannot be moved once placed. Imprisoned pieces may only be saved by a player's Dungeon Explorer.
- **DUNGEON EXPLORER** - A character with maps and schematics of the Dungeon that can save entrapped pieces over the course of 20 turns.
- **ARCH MAGE** - This mysterious figure wields the power of a magical secret and may drastically alter the course of the game at a moment's notice. He is considered neutral, and controlled by neither player, entering the game at his own will.

Dungeon, Dungeon Explorer, Arch Mage

Understand the rules and the pieces? Simple enough, right?

Your Mentor's Death and Subsequent Existence as a Ghostly Spectre

The doorbell rings. Your mother answers it and calls for you.

"The police are here," she says, "and they have some questions for you. Did you do something wrong?"

"Son," they say, in the living room. "We've heard you're quite the Chess buff?"

"I am."

"Then we have some bad news."

How He Died

In order for your mentor to be with you for all eternity and watch over your every game move, he must unfortunately pass away. We need to define the last thread of the powerful bond with your mentor:

A Vague but Terrible Sickness: Something the doctors could neither diagnose nor cure and which escalated throughout the last days of his life. If this is how your mentor died, there's a recurring suspicion that his sickness was, in fact, poison.

Preventing a Violent Crime and Dying a Hero: Regardless of which character type your mentor was, there were times when you wondered why he had such a cruel side. You'll never forget how small he made you feel when you tried to castle your way out of check. Then, this man with his cruel and impatient tendencies gave himself for a stranger's life.

Death at the Chess Table: Lots of ways for this to go down, but the most common are either cardiac arrest or a stabbing.

Disappeared, Only to Reappear a Corpse in a Body of Water Weeks Later: Up to you whether it was a lake, ocean, river, or swimming pool.

Disappeared, Only to Reappear as a Corpse in a Suburban Dungeon: Your mentor had many enemies. One of them may have paid an assassin to have him kidnapped and imprisoned in a subterranean lair where he died in either an attempt to escape or by self-poisoning (it's possible that your mentor always carried cyanide for situations such as this.)

The Ghost Part

When did your mentor first appear to you in spectral form? Was it immediately after his death? Or was it a presence that began quietly, through something like the scent of his patchouli oil or cologne appearing in a room next to a Chess board? Or an unexplained warmth in a cold room?

Does the ghost stand behind you as you play, or beside you? Does the ghost speak or does it only gesture with its eyes? Does it carry a reminder of the wounds he sustained in his death?

Do you win games because your ghostly mentor is there encouraging you? Or do you lose them, choking under the presence of this spirit?

CREATING YOUR CHESS STRATEGY

A frail transparent hand points to the enemy's Bishop. But why? It seems harmless now, but if your mentor's spectre is pointing it out, that Bishop could spell trouble later. Best to take it out while you have the chance!

Which piece to play, and when? This is going to hinge largely on which mentor you chose.

If your mentor was the Cool Guy in the Park, then you will play slapdash, intimidating, with bravado and distraction. Better to move the piece quickly than to linger. Better to cause a mistake in your opponent by making them rush than to give them time and space.

The Stuffy Academic would have you play correctly, with panache but restraint. Stick to the classics. Develop your skill set. Learn the fundamentals and use them. Tuck your shirt in and comb your hair.

Then there is the Mysterious Russian. He played with fury and intimidation. He always sought first blood and made his enemies—and you—weep with terror.

Then, color each initial strategy with the cryptic signals you receive from beyond the grave.

The Game

Knock knock. It's years later and you're back in your present time, ready to finally play some Chess. You look to the door and your opponent knocks again.

Knock knock.

Who came to play this evening?

The difficulty of opponent you choose will determine the style and length of the game. It will also decide whether you pull out all the stops, or go easy. What kind of game would you like to play tonight?

The easiest mode of play is against a precocious young neighborhood boy named Young Benjamin. Benjamin is a ten-year-old, the single child of your next-door neighbors, Philip and Diane. His parents sought you out because of your reputation and your status as the final student of your deceased mentor. They want Benjamin to learn from the best.

Benjamin doesn't know the rules

The first challenge in playing against young Benjamin is prying his eyes away from his *Wilbur the Warthog* handheld video game, and focusing on the game that you want to play, instead. You've noticed he has a tendency to play games alone, outside, which means that he's a good companion for something more sociable. (It also could indicate that the boy should own a copy of the very book you hold in your hands right now.)

Phillip and Diane also will invite themselves over tonight to watch the game see how it goes. They will sit in the corner of the room, sharing a bottle of wine—making it quite the full house, especially when you consider that the ghost of your mentor is also present in the room (although this is unbeknownst to Benjamin or his parents.)

An additional challenge is that Philip and Diane are rather hands-off during Chess time, leaving the discipline and gamesmanship to you. Benjamin's loose grasp on the rules leads to many mistakes, which you may misinterpret as cheating. While, at times, this can remind you of your own childhood tomfoolery (and perhaps illicit a wry smile out of your spectral mentor), it serves as a frustrating and unforeseen element.

Giving this temperamental young boy some slack is the best way to let this game run smoothly and maintain a decent relationship with your neighbors—but it can also set you up for a game that ends in defeat.

INTERMEDIATE: ANGELA

Angela has much in store...

You first met Angela during college, when she was a sophisticated postgraduate student. The two of you met in the campus Chess club, spending your nights staying up late and laughing, always finding one another a formidable match. Your Chess skills have stayed much the same over the years, making this a truly even Chess game.

But there is something different when Angela arrives tonight. She looks teary-eyed. The bottle of Malbec you bought for this evening— a bottle you spent an entire ten dollars on—may go unopened, you realize, when she tells you that this might be the last time the two of you play against one another.

Over the years, your love for her remained unannounced but known. A presence that hung in the air.

"I am moving to Paris," she says.

"Wow. I've never been to Europe before. Only in my daydreams."

"Maybe you can visit me someday? Now, let's play one last game."

Your mentor stands in the corner. He does not speak—as he rarely ever speaks—but you know what he thinks. Will you finally tell her how you feel? Will you convince her to stay? Will you drop everything and uproot your life to be closer to her?

And will you be able to win this game of Chess?

DIFFICULT: THE MACHINE

Lightning crackles in the air, and a dark silhouette stands outside your front door. *Ding dong.* It is here.

They told you about this machine at the local Chess club and you could not help but be intrigued. Do not trust it, they said. Do not invite it into your home. It's practically a walking fax machine, a strange entity made for one purpose alone and that purpose is to play Chess.

145

The Machine has no emotions

With every game it plays, it knows more and plays better. Some call it cheating. Others call it science.

It's just a machine, you might say. Yes, but it is a machine that knocked on your door and walked into your home and now sits across from you at a Chess board. A robot, a man of tin, a creature made by man that has become more than the men or the machines that breathed life into it.

Like Frankenstein's monster-child, this creature that sits before you is a beast, yet a beast for whom you feel sadness and empathy. It wishes itself both dead and to know a better life all at once.

Your mentor shudders at the sight of it. It disgusts him too greatly, this clicking nightmare. Your mentor thusly leaves the room when the machine arrives, for it is the only thing that scares him.

You cannot weep for it, of course, regardless of how sad its empty life makes you. You must defeat it instead.

EXPERT: THE SHADOW

A ghostly wind blows through the room. But it is not your mentor.

Instead, a dark aura conjures itself across from you, taking the form a seated person—a form not unlike your own. This opponent will test your Chess skills and your sanity.

A rift in the Shadow Realm

There is something harder to defeat than the Machine. Something terrible and frightening.

Your Shadow Self, of course. Sitting across the table, once again.

But when you think about it, it always has been your Shadow Self, hasn't it? The one that plays all these games with you, here to play one more.

The rules of Chess you have learned may not apply tonight, however. Under such intense pressure, you may wish to forget trying to defeat the Shadow Self and stand up to sit alongside it. Then, and only then, can you play—and defeat—the ghostly mentor who still haunts you.

It's your decision: team up with the Ghost against the Shadow, or the Shadow against the Ghost. Tread carefully. The last thing you need is for the Ghost and the Shadow to join forces against you. You will stand no chance of defeating them when combined.

Who is Ready for Chess Time?

It is now up to you to carry on this ancient tradition and uphold or destroy your mentor's legacy. Get out your Chess board. Lay down the pieces in the indicated order (or in any order you see fit.) Summon the ghostly visage of your deceased mentor and pray that you will not face him at this table tonight.

Your doorbell rings, and you must answer it.

Ghostly mentor by your side?

Remember the rules?

GO!

ANOTHER LIFE

THE SUN RISES OVER YELLOW WINDSWEPT FIELDS OF GRAIN,

the soft reds and striking yellows streaking across the sky, piercing through the fading night, bringing new life to this forgotten corner of America. Birds chirp, chittering and chattering, announcing the arrival of another day.

You breathe in, deeply, and bring your hand to the spot of your cable-knit sweater that has soaked through with blood. You raise the fingers and inspect them, there, in the nascent dawn. The bullet has done its damage although you feel no pain.

What if, you wonder. What if you had taken another path that would have avoided this fate?

Yet even this path—the botched robbery, the untrustworthy jewel thief, the tragedy of your life—was meant to be a new path of its own. Even this you had meant to be that one thing so many people crave, that chance to right your wrongs, to live it all again: another life.

And so you slip from your pocket something you've carried with you all these years, something that has been by your side through thick and thin: a copy of your favorite book, Games You Can Play In Your Head, By Yourself.

> Shed all your regrets and woes, all your lost hopes and dreams,
> and step into **ANOTHER LIFE!**

This may be the simplest game in my compendium.

It might also be the hardest.

This game requires a deeper look at life than most humans are capable of. It will force you to look deeply at both your own quiet life and those of the souls of strangers.

The Rules

The good thing about this game is that, like many near-impossible things, the rules break down into these simple steps:

I. Choose a life.
II. Take that life for yourself.
III. Live that life until a **Logical Conclusion** has been reached or a **Lesson** has been learned.
IV. Firmly eject yourself from that life, landing back into reality (where you are now).

The third step is most important with a game like this. While most of the games I've invented have fantastical or otherworldly elements which will cue most players to the nature of their false reality, this game does not. Once you begin living them, they might be indistinguishable from your own.

Do not be greedy. Do not waste these lives. Relinquish the life when your lesson has been learned and return to yourself.

It's crucial to remember that your actual life in this reality is the most valuable one of them all, despite its shortcomings. Ideally, once you have experienced *Another Life*, you will return to your own with a renewed and profound sense of appreciation.

150

How to Choose a Life

In order to play Another Life, you have to first examine your own life and consider what is missing and then determine how imagining another life would solve what's missing.

So, briefly—in thirty seconds or fewer—consider what elements of your life are dissatisfactory. Are you bored by your schoolwork or your job? Your living quarters? Your personal relationships?

Choose a life that is substantially different or more exciting than your own. Here are a few possibilities for people who might have such lives:

A FAMOUS ATHLETE

Think of the most famous athlete you can. What makes his or her life so good? How many awards have they won? How many admiring fans do they have? What would your body feel like after achieving what they have?

But careful: you'll have to play the sport if you do take on this life, and that could be tough!

A POPULAR MUSICIAN

Is there a musician you wish you could be? One whose skin you would love to wear? One whose lifestyle you could keep up with? Do they have cool hair? What famous songs do you wish you could play or take credit for writing?

Careful! If you decide to take on the life of a musician who is struggling with crippling addictions, impostor syndrome, or an overwhelming sense of loneliness, that will become *your* rock to push!

THE POPE

Sure, at first, being the Pope might sound like a hopeless nightmare. Imagine being a celibate dying man living in a fortress in Rome, surrounded by physical riches that add no substance or joy to your life. There could be a good element, however: you may have a direct line to a supreme deity. If you have a plan to harness that power, the world could be yours.

Old Sly Willy

Remember this old bastard? What you don't know about him will surprise you. Turns out he's got:

- A cool car collection
- A time-share in Key West
- A beautiful wife, Esmerelda
- A bar in his finished basement
- A stuffed antelope head on the wall by the bar, which he killed

A Tiger

Rooooooooooooarrrrrrrrrrrrrr!

Now you're an animal. It also could be any animal, not just tigers.

Watch out for poachers!

A Warrior-Toad

Explore Earth as a being from another planet! But meanwhile, cope with the stoic loneliness of knowing you'll never see your homeland again and the baggage of being a brave emissary who forages forward with neither friend nor lover.

You can also jump really high!

Time Traveler With Futuristic Technology In the Modern Day

Dark and brooding with mysterious origins, you can only sit by and watch as humanity is doomed to repeat the mistakes that created the brutal timeline you've come from.

Bumbling Time Traveler From the Past In The Modern Day

Is this what humanity has come to? How has the future strayed so far from the traditions of your time? Everyone acts silly, rude, or downright ignorant, and only you know that the problems of today require the solutions from yesterday.

Were the ones before this not exciting or substantially different enough? Perhaps you want to play as yourself. Perhaps the life you currently live is not the one meant for you.

Inside each and every one of us burns the deep scars of regret. Decisions that were made in haste, conversations with words not meant to be spoken. Lovers that have betrayed you—or ones you have betrayed yourself.

Pinpoint a devastating moment and then turn back the clock to find a new path. Or for an added challenge: wipe the whole slate clean and start from scratch as a newborn! It's up to you.

They say we only live once. Maybe, this time, you don't.

Taking Another Life for Yourself

There are one of two ways to begin living one of these lives: either jump right in at birth or find a pivotal moment from which to become the other being.

This is easy enough, unless you are playing as yourself—which I recommend, as it's one of the most challenging.

If you'd like to play as yourself, it's easiest to consider your life in its entirety as if you lie upon your death bed. Shy away from nothing. Examine all of it, every last moment. Dwell on regret and heartache and pain.

Then, choose a catalyzing moment from your life and consider how you would have made a different decision in that moment.

You can also do this if playing as someone other than yourself, but in that case you should be sure to fully consider all the joys and regrets of this other being—for example, what did Old Sly Willy wish he'd done instead of going into trucking? Did the Tiger in the forest wish it had eaten more antelopes?

If you struggle with finding a moment, here are some examples that may jog your memory or inspire new sparks and flames:

- The friend who went swimming, with whom you could have gone too and who never returned from the quarry that day
- The day you let a bully torment a weaker student and never stepped in

- The last job interview you failed--whether last week or four decades ago
- The time you had the opportunity to prevent a friend from shoplifting but chose not to
- The first job interview you failed
- When you didn't chase your love and move to Paris
- Missing your first child's birth
- Also, missing your second child's
- Third child, too
- Et cetera

The list can go on and on but here's the tough part: you can only choose one regrettable moment, per game.

Choose wisely.

Finding A Lesson or Logical Conclusions In Life

Remember, all roads lead through life to one location. At the end, we all pay the same reaper. That's why you should aim to either learn a **Lesson** from that life or reach a **Logical Conclusion** within it. But what's the difference between the two?

Logical Conclusions are goals, successes, failures that are relative to only the inhabited life, and are meant only to provide entertainment.

Lessons are the deeper moments and stories that bear resemblance to challenges you face in your own life, and the parallels provide guidance for how you should act in reality (where you are now).

Here are some examples of the Lessons and Logical Conclusions you can look for in life:

LOGICAL CONCLUSIONS

- Motorcycle racer wants to win the big race, wins, then crashes and dies.
- Fat boy who eats sweets one day owns Ice Cream factory and becomes rich and then dies.
- Man who spends all his time playing video games becomes digitized and trapped in said game, dies in real life, but still alive in video game.

154

- Dead mummy who sleeps all day finally awakens when intruder enters pyramid, but is slashed to bits by Adventurer's sword, finding eternal peace.
- Dungeon keeper keeps Dungeon at 100% capacity for his life span, then in his final days imprisoned by his paranoid Dungeon Lord, dies with the same agony he subjected others to.
- Man with no job gets job, dies
- Bad child with bad grades is promised a reward for good grades, steals reward. Gets in trouble.
- Good child with bad grades is promised a reward for good grades, gets good grades and is rewarded. Dies.
- Tiger wants antelope, finds said antelope, dies.
- Toad-like creature from distant planet travels to Earth and finds child companion. Dies.
- Truck driver realizes he has wasted life, has epiphany, races home to share with family, crashes, dies.

LESSONS

Look out for these life Lessons:

- Don't steal.
- Don't lie.
- Don't be bad.
- Family is important.
- Don't trust strangers.
- Losing friends is easy, making them is hard.
- The easy road is usually the hard road.
- The hard road is usually a slow road.
- All roads lead to the reaper.
- Love is a highway and sometimes you need to pull off to the shoulder.
- You're a combination of the five people you spend the most time in the car with.
- Never eat raw hamburger meat.
- Sometimes eating other raw meats is worth it.
- Drugs are extremely dangerous.
- Don't be jealous.
- Compare yourself only to who you were yesterday, not to others as they are today.

Don't Lose The Horizon

The realm of shadows is elusive... but when found, it can be so seductive that many who enter it never return.

The greatest danger in any of my games is that you lose yourself and never find your way back to reality. Like Theseus in the labyrinth, you must always keep one hand on your ball of twine if you are ever to retrace your steps and escape.

Please, be careful. Do not disappear so far into Another Life—or any of my thousands of games—that you are unable to return.

If you play this game right, you will walk back into Your Life with a sense of optimism and joy. If you play it wrong, you could live in Another Life forever.

Editors' Note: *We cannot echo this sentiment strongly enough. Enjoy one of the best games we've collected so far! Fun stuff!*

Ready?

Go!

EPILOGUE: OPEN THE TREASURE BOX

THE ENDLESS PLANES OF INFINITY CONVERGE INTO ONE.

Each game distills a realm of possibilities into a single dimension borne from your decisions.

And with treasures in hand, there is but one destination left to go.

With dutiful repetition, you find yourself walking through a field once more. You look down and see your shadow, cast from the sun shining down on your body, darkness upon the grains of wheat, matching the outline of your body.

You know your shadow well and you always have. Your shadow walks with you, a dark reflection, a fellow self.

You reach a building here in the field. The building should be something of your choice. Remember? You have conjured it up: a barn, a cottage, an abandoned house, a mill or a burned-down castle or a lonely tower.

But now other lives have been lived, and souvenirs gained. Maybe a lion's claw lodged in your side from combat, which you now pull out with your teeth. Even a gold medal that has been won from your extraordinary leaping abilities. Perhaps a dirty paper napkin, that when opened, reveals a phone number that you have yet to call. Or even a sparkle of fairy dust, that when observed, reminds you of a conversation you wish you could have again.

It is now time to place your final souvenir amongst your other Treasures within your Sanctuary. Each one collected is to play a part in your final experience.

Find it. March towards it.

And within your **Treasure Box** you will find something astounding:

One of the items you have placed in your Treasure Box is now missing.

You might want to double check the *notes* section of this book, to confirm that it is indeed gone. Because it most certainly *is.*

Which item has it taken?

It is abundantly clear that it is your Shadow Self that is to blame.

Did it take something of great value, that you hoped would bring you wealth?

Did it take something sentimental, a reminder of the joyful adventures you once had?

Did you take something back to your Sanctuary that you should not have?

Or, was it something you could not get rid of on your own?

A burden whose weight has finally been lifted?

Of course, only I know what it was. I took it for myself.

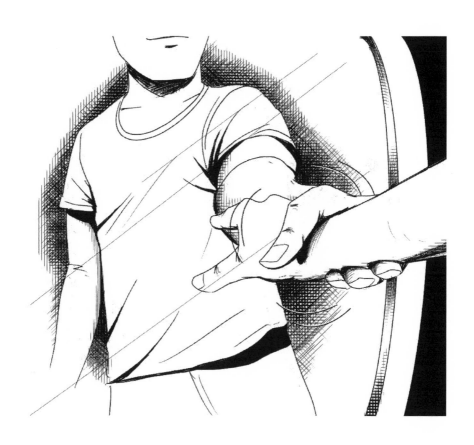

Which item did I covet most?

Which item would l be willing to steal?

Why would I steal it?

What game am l playing?

Why am I by myself, in my own head?

TOP TEN GAMES YOU CAN PLAY IN YOUR HEAD, BY YOURSELF

BY J. THEOPHRASTUS BARTHOLOMEW

EDITED BY SAM GORSKI AND D. F. LOVETT

ORIGINAL ARTWORK BY GABRIEL PEREGRINO

ABOUT THE AUTHOR

In an explosion of creativity, J. Theophrastus Bartholomew originally published his fourteen-volume groundbreaking series *Games You Can Play In Your Head, By Yourself* between 1988 and 1993.

Each volume of the original series contains the same photograph of the author, likely taken during the time of his life when he began creating his first games. It is reproduced below.

Due to his use of a pen name, *J. Theophrastus Bartholomew,* specific details of Bartholomew's life remain unknown, including whether he is alive and still writing today. However, we're able to confidently assume—between the photo and the information provided to us from the original publisher—that he was born in Minnesota in the late 1960s or early 1970s.

ABOUT THE EDITORS

Sam Gorski and D. F. Lovett are lifelong friends who first met at Stillwater Junior High School during the filming of *The Alabine Armor*, a *Star Wars* fan film. They instantly bonded over their love of roleplaying games and fantasy fiction.

D. F. Lovett is a writer and author whose works include *The Moonborn: or, Moby-Dick on the Moon* and several forthcoming works of science fiction.

Sam Gorski is a filmmaker and musician who co-founded Corridor Digital, a popular online destination for short films. This is his first published work.

Acknowledgements

Thank you to everyone who helped make this book happen! We appreciate the support of our friends, family, and, of course, the rest of the Corridor Digital team who indulged this momentous project of editing and research.

Thank you to our loved ones who supported us throughout this project, especially Sarah Gorski and Molly Long.

Of course, a special *thank you* is due to the family who chose to sell their copies of *Games You Can Play In Your Head, By Yourself* at their yard sale in the summer of 2014. Without that we would have never discovered what would become one of our great passions.

We appreciate the generosity of the original publisher who, while unable to put us in touch with J. Theophrastus Bartholomew, was able to lawfully transfer the rights of the game series to us so we could share it with the world.

Finally, this book owes its existence to the brilliant mind of J. Theophrastus Bartholomew. If you read this, Mr. Bartholomew, and you would like to get in touch, please know that we would love to hear from you and share our plans to release future editions and volumes.

SAM GORSKI AND D. F. LOVETT

APPENDIX: The Stories of Those Who Played Before You

As we moved forward with compiling this book, one thing we learned was that it can be helpful to learn the experiences of others. Usually it is best to learn these **after** you've already played a game at least once, which is why we didn't include them earlier.

But, if you're stalled out in a game—or not sure how to start, or why, or can't tell when you are finished—then these gameplay testimonials could be helpful for you.

As you read, ask yourself how your adventure compares. Was it as exciting as these? Feel free to jot down some thoughts so that you don't forget.

The Stories of Those Who Played "Adventure" Before You

- **Seth:** "I was really scared, especially when I met the Demon Nazi who was guarding my great-grandmother's ashes. He kept flinging scorpions at me from a bucket and I really thought I was going to die. The only way I made it through was by drawing on my childhood memory of being lost in the hills of Scotland, where a ghost girl taught me spells that weaken undead beings. Next time I play Adventure, I'll be sure to properly prepare for how scary it gets."
- **Carmen:** "I was bored for a little bit because I got drunk with Hassan after we met the Mapmaker and then couldn't find my way back to the hotel. I think I burned a lot of time on that. Then I got lost again

below the pyramids. It ended up being really exciting as soon as I did find the hedge maze inside the underground cavern of Cromandies the Red. Sadly, I lost in my final battle against him.
- **Salvatore**: "It was a mistake to try to play as a Nazi. My guilt overcame me so profoundly that I had to bail on the entire adventure and seek redemption by becoming an American spy. They refused me and I ended up going to prison. When I stopped playing the game, I was still awaiting my sentencing."
- **Lee**: "This was awesome. I killed so many mummies and then brought the haunted crystal broach back to the Museum of Natural History."

The Stories of Those Who Played "Space" Before You

- **Chris N**: "I decided I would help smuggle spice from one end of the galaxy to the other. It was really cool and I even flew my spaceship straight through the Sun and lived."
- **Tim L**: "I crashed my spaceship when I was trying to take off and someone called the police and they came and arrested me. The media labeled it the Trial of the Decade and I became known as the Spaceship Man. All of that was pretty interesting but I think I would've rather explored space."

The Stories of Those Who Played "Dungeons" Before You

- **Christopher**: "Christ, I thought I was gonna starve to death down there."
- **Mark**: "I played as a Dungeon Explorer with a penchant for killing evil creatures and I spent a ton of time lost, trying to find the vampire that I was fairly certain lived somewhere in those eerie tunnels. Eventually I found a coffin and pried it open, ready to kill the beast in its heart, but then I realized it was actually occupied by a different Dungeon Explorer who was just taking a nap in the coffin. He was really cool about it and we ended up exploring further, until he got decapitated by the Dungeon Keeper. After that, I just bailed. I'm sure there's cool stuff down there but I couldn't really take it anymore. Creepy vibes."
- **Joe T**: "I really didn't want to do anything big in the Dungeons. I thought it would be best to be a low key Dungeon dude who didn't

really mess with anyone else and just minded my own business, but then a Frankenstein monster came and dismembered me."

- <u>Ricky</u>: "I've never been big into fantasy, so I played this one as a Dungeon Lord and stayed above ground the whole time. The Dungeon Keeper I hired wouldn't stop bothering me with updates on the Dungeon's construction, and so eventually stopped coming to me with updates all together. By the time I decided to check in on the progress below, I was surprised to learn that they ended up not completing it because they went over budget, and the whole thing ended up as a logistical nightmare."

The Stories of Those Who Played "Trucks" Before You

- <u>Carter</u>: "I can't wrap my head around how many family birthdays I missed."
- <u>Kurt</u>: "The monster truck was by far my favorite, although it took me a few years of game time to earn my way up to driving it. I got really good at transporting oranges by dragging them in a wagon behind the monster truck. What I did was build lots of jumps around the country then I would go off the jump and basically fly from coast to coast by hitting the jumps just right. I saved a ton of time that way."
- <u>Ivy B</u>: "I stopped playing when I killed so many pedestrians that every cop in America was trying to chase me down. It just stopped being worth it, trying to get from city to city with that much heat on my tail."
- <u>Steve</u>: "I got murdered at a brothel. I worry my death brought shame to all my families."
- <u>Casper</u>: "I cut some corners and started driving a semi-truck that just wasn't up to snuff. Old Sly Willy always pestered me for repairs, dealing with flat tires and break-downs, leaky oil tanks, etc, but I never had time to visit the shop to fix them. This also made me more prone to carjackers, which there seemed to be a lot of."

The Stories of Those Who Played "The Visitor" Before You

- <u>Pat L</u>: "I found Drexxel in Knighthell. He actually seemed to not really mind it too much, so we really had to woo him hard to come back to the physical plane."

- **Niko P:** "Nighthell was by far the worst experience of my life. I lived something like two eternities there with Chadpole until the 'darkness' finally overcame him. I escaped once I found one of the fallen spears of light, which had been lost to time and buried like six miles beneath the sea of black ash. Definitely the best game in this book."
- **Sarah G:** "My summer vacation was pretty great. I really had fun working for my dad's trucking company, and all my friends came to my birthday party. I'm kind of sad my mom didn't let me sleep in the tent the rest of the summer. Weird."
- **Gabe P:** "Don't hate me for this, but the Viktorians have a pretty good reason to exterminate those toads. Those fucking toads ruined my summer!"

The Stories of Those Who Played "The Alamo" Before You

- **Lauren:** "I joined up with the gold rush pretty quickly. Not much appeal in being at the actual Battle of the Alamo. Sounds like a nightmare honestly. But some of the other time travel stuff was cool."
- **John:** "I think Santa Anna was right. It was cool to get to tell him that to his face."
- **Nick G:** "Have you ever had your whole body sunburned? Finding a disguise was way more difficult than I thought it would be."
- **Sean:** "In the midst of the battle, that other time traveler guy caught up with me and it turns out he was pretty cool. Turns out he was me from a previous time travel expedition, researching the Alamo from 1835. He realized he was way in over his head, and decided to lay low until someone else came to save him. We made a great team in defeating the Alamo once and for all, prematurely abolishing slavery."

The Stories of Those Who Played "Murder Night" Before You

- **Brad:** "I think I assassinated the wrong person. I'm almost certain I did. It was with the revolver, but not the one I brought with me. I stole someone else's revolver and planted it on the butler. I think the police will have a pretty tough time tracing it back to me, which is nice."
- **Justin:** "I realized that I could just poison the soup and kill everyone, because I'd been murdering for an Extraordinarily Long Time. I feel a

little guilty about it now that I'm back in reality but it seemed like a fail-safe way to ensure the target was dead."

- **Sally**: "I listened in on a conversation between Bucky Barlowe and Zephyr Xanadu and it sounded like Barlowe is involved in child slavery. This suggests that, even if he wasn't the original target, he deserves to die. That, and anyone mixed up in child slavery has a few demons and many enemies. So I went to the kitchen, found some arsenic, and walked back into the party with a wine glass. The trouble is, when I tried to hand it to him, he revealed that he doesn't drink wine. So I had to go back into the kitchen, get more arsenic, and make him a lemonade. At this point, people noticed that I was going into the kitchen, which was a faux pas, and that I was really insistent on giving Barlowe a drink. I screwed up, basically. I had to come clean at the end of the night and admit what I was trying to do. They ended up being pretty forgiving about it."
- **Jacki**: "The moment I arrived at the party, I was insulted by Standor Stephenson. He mocked my shoes, for being unpolished and scuffed. So I killed him with a wrench when the power went out and hid his body under the sofa. Then I realized he wasn't the target, because I discovered the parchment was in fact in pocket the whole time, and I was just not digging deep enough. Make sure you check your pockets at least three times!"

The Stories of Those Who Played "Your Job" Before You

- **David**: "I started the game pretty firmly resistant to the machines, but I was rather wooed by them by the end. If we play our cards right, this should lead to a better life for everyone, rather than scarcity or starvation. People are too limited in their views of automation and artificial intelligence. That said, one of the robots has been bullying me throughout town and it's getting pretty weird."
- **Jake W**: "I mean, I'm already a little biased against robots. I figured I would be best at welding, and plus it would give me the best chances against fighting off robots with my cutting tools. This proved a pretty good strategy but ultimately they overwhelmed me and took my job."
- **Tommy G**: "So I was a mover but I was replaced pretty quickly. But then I got a crazy idea and decided to show up to work the next day with Zoop Zoops taped to my face and made it to retirement."

The Stories of Those Who Played "Chess" Before You

- **Nick L**: "I was actually in Chess club in high school, so I was pretty confident going into this game. I decided to play the expert opponent and summon my Shadow Self, but when he showed up there was this tinier Shadow Self with him. Two Shadow Selves. I thought it was weird, so I didn't say anything. We sat down to play chess, and before I could even make my first move, the tiny Shadow Self pulled out a tiny knife and stabbed me in the stomach, and I died. I guess I lost."
- **Dutch**: "My mentor was like the father I never had. It makes me weep to think of him, his body riddled with bullet holes, floating in a pond. Thing is, two detectives came and interrupted my chess date with Angela to tell me that they finally cracked the case and that it turns out he wasn't murdered by bullets. They were fired into his dead body. He had drowned in there and then some neighborhood kids used his body for target practice, or at least that's the working theory. Anyway, I think that this gave my mentor, Julian, the closure he never had. His ghostly presence listened attentively to the detectives as they spoke of his cold case and then, at the end of their tale, he slowly faded away. I can still remember his presence in life but it has started to feel like the ghost that followed me for the past two decades was never really there. I hope this means he is free and can finally move on from the spectral plane."
- **Steve**: "I lost to Benjamin three times in a row. I guess I'm not very good at chess."

The Stories of Those Who Played "Another Life" Before You

- **Frank**: "I walk through the blank walls of my own life like a stranger in the body of my dead twin. So yeah, pretty good game, I guess."
- **Molly**: "I played as the tiger!"
- **Carmichael D**: "I peed my pants in 6th grade - totally an accident - and it set me off on a pretty toxic course for middle school. So I went back, regulated my fluids a bit better, and now I'm a lawyer! Or at least I was in the game."
- **Danny G**: "I lived as a nomad in the desert for seventeen years, but when I woke up, found it was only two days in real time. What happened was that I forgot how to snap myself out of the game, went on a search for answers, ended up getting lost in an infinite desert,

where I eventually found an imaginary copy of the book. When I opened it, I expected to find some sort of instructions on how to wake up, but it was blank. The shock of hopelessness was actually so severe that it snapped me out of it, saving my life."

NOTES

187

191

37789851R00118

Made in the USA
Middletown, DE
02 March 2019